A PARENT'S GUIDE TO BALANCE AND GETTING MORE YOU TIME

JACKIE HALL

Disclaimer: The intent of this author is only to offer information of a general nature to help you in your quest for emotional well-being. It is not intended to be a substitute for any psychological, financial, legal, or any other professional advice. In the event you use any of the information in this book for yourself, the author and publisher assume no responsibility for your actions. If expert assistance or counselling is needed, the services of a competent medical or psychological professional should be sought.

First published 2013

© 2013 Jackie Hall

All rights reserved. Without limiting the rights under copyright restricted above, no part of this publication may be reproduced, stored in or introduced into a retrieval system, or transmitted, in any form or by any means (electronic, mechanical, photocopying, recording or otherwise), without the prior written permission of both the copyright owner and the above publisher of this book.

Designed and typeset by Vicki Gauci

Cover design by Roland Ali Pantin
Edited by Louise Johnson

ISBN 978 0 9875433 1 8

Table of Contents

A parent's guide to time management and getting more 'me' time 1

Time management is not about Time 4

The Mind TRACK to Happiness process 12

Upgrading the four stressful thinking lenses 23

Applying the upgrades 35

Exercise One: What do I do with My Time? 38

What is really important to me? 41

Exercise Two: What's important to me? 42

Getting Organised 45

Exercise Three – Making lists 52

Exercise Four – Establishing what I want 54

Exercise Five – How do I get what I want? 57

Exercise Six – Create your own time schedule 69

Part B – Time Out 73

Readjusting your idea of time out 77

Step One: Thoughts 80

Allowing yourself to take time out 85

Why you deserve time out 89

The benefits of taking time out 91

The different types of time out 96

Time Out for the Soul 102

Conclusion 109

A Parent's Guide To Balance *And Getting More 'You' Time.*

A parent's guide to time management and getting more 'me' time.

Somewhere underneath the massive pile of washing, the endless sea of household chores, homework, play dates, after school activities, during school activities, work, bills, your social life, quiet time, quality time and everything else that needs to be done "yesterday", you may find a frazzled, worn out parent who is trying to do it all.

The pressure to do everything and at the same time raise healthy, happy, well rounded children without getting overwhelmed, losing the plot and feeling like the worst parent in the world, is huge.

However, when I come across a parent who is consumed, stressed and sometimes anxious due to all the demands of being a parent, there is always much more going on behind the scenes than just the circumstances of a busy life.

There's no doubt most of us are getting busier and our 'to do' list continues to get longer. Sometimes it seems just as we finish a task, like house cleaning, it's time to start all over again.

Our goal posts keep moving. The pressure to achieve perfection is mounting, which is causing an epidemic of

A Parent's Guide To Balance *And Getting More 'You' Time.*

stress and anxiety as we continually try to get life right and feel depressed when we can't.

Something needs to change. Society's emphasis on getting more, doing more and having more in order to feel more successful means the pressure is only getting worse.

The Parent's Guide to Time Management and Getting More 'Me' Time is much more than a 'how to organise yourself' guide.

You probably purchased this book with the intention of learning how to manage your time, but like everything at the Parental Stress Centre, we're going to look beyond the surface of your stress and teach you how to overcome your stress about time issues first, then we'll compliment that newfound knowledge with an action plan

Your 'to do' list is just that – a list of things to do. But often you don't see it that way. You see it as a 'must do right now or else' list and when you start clinging to something you believe you 'must' do but can't, stress comes in.

This book will help you integrate some fun back into your life – you know, to actually enjoy your life and not feel like you've signed up for a day in, day out boot camp.

You're going to learn how to stop feeling stressed or anxious when you can't get things done and to be okay about letting things on your list go at times.

A Parent's Guide To Balance *And Getting More 'You' Time.*

You will learn how to approach your busy life with clarity, focus and an ability to prioritise according to what you hold really important, rather than what you feel you HAVE to do.

Most importantly this book will teach you how to relax and enjoy the moment without getting caught up in it.

Sure there will always be menial, boring tasks to do in life, but this book will help you change the way you view those tasks and avoid getting consumed by them to the point of exhaustion.

That's not what life is about and that's not the attitude you want your children to be seeing or learning either.

It's time to step into a more balanced, happier and more fulfilling way to live your life as a parent.

A Parent's Guide To Balance *And Getting More 'You' Time.*

Time management is not about Time

"Prepare to be set free as you learn the watch words of time management. Guess what?

Neither of them is time or management. The need-to-know magic words are Choice and Focus."

(Source: Time management for Manic Mums; Allison Mitchell: 2006)

Time Management is not actually all about managing your time, it's about managing your priorities.

That's what Allison Mitchell refers to as choice and focus.

What do I choose to focus on doing with my time?

This may seem like a very simple question, however the answer is somewhat more intricate. This is because the word "choice" is largely misunderstood.

Let's consider this example:

"I want to have some time out and read a book or go and play a round of golf, but I have household chores that need doing that I've been putting off for weeks. Which option do I choose?"

Well this depends on what your beliefs are about each option and what you think it means about you as a person when you choose one option over the other.

A Parent's Guide To Balance *And Getting More 'You' Time.*

To understand why you choose to do one thing with your time and not another, a journey into the way humans think is necessary.

How we make decisions

On page 6 there is a diagram of how every human thinks:

- a) First an event occurs;
- b) We experience that event with one or more of the five senses (sight, sound, touch, taste or smell);
- c) The brain goes into an evaluation process. It looks for an understanding of what the information coming from the senses actually means. The brain searches through all of the information that has come from all of your experiences of life to date and tries to link what you are sensing with information that will help you understand what it means.

  - What is it?
  - Have I seen it before?
  - Do I have an opinion about it?
  - Do I have a past experience or reference point for it?
  - What am I supposed to do about it?

A Parent's Guide To Balance *And Getting More 'You' Time.*

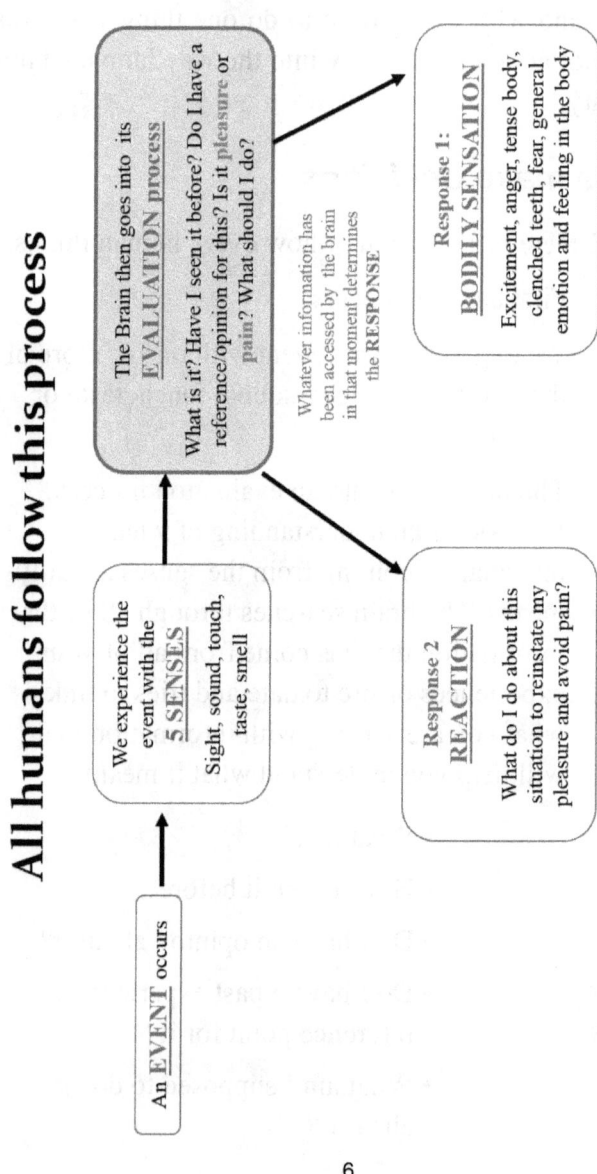

A Parent's Guide To Balance *And Getting More 'You' Time.*

The brain does this evaluation automatically. Mostly it is done with the subconscious part of the brain. You may be aware of some of the monologue going on in your mind, but certainly not all of it. You aren't aware of the almost immediate sifting and linking of information that occurs in a split second.

Imagine the enormity of your brain's task to sift through all of the information stored from the beginning of your time on earth, in search for what a particular event means… and on a moment to moment basis. Wow! The brain sure is a remarkable organ.

On top of that, the brain is always searching for an understanding of *'what does this event mean about me as a person?"*

This is the primal concern of a human being and it comes from an innate instinct to seek pleasure and avoid pain (ie feel good and not feel bad). Therefore it's really important for the brain to establish what it is you're experiencing just in case you need to do something about it quick.

For example, what if a spider was to land on your shoulder? Very quickly the brain links the information from your eyes to the label 'spider' (because I've seen a spider before and have learnt that this picture I'm seeing is linked to the label spider) and also links to the belief you hold about spiders that you've also learnt from your experience of life. "Spiders can hurt you (inflict pain)".

A Parent's Guide To Balance *And Getting More 'You' Time.*

In order to avoid pain and maintain the equilibrium of a pain-free, feel good life, the brain very quickly determines that it needs to get the spider off your shoulder... now!

We then reach the next step of the evaluation process – The Response:

    a)   The response process happens in two ways

        i)   The Mind body connection – the bodily response. The brain sends information to the body instructing it how to react based on how the brain has perceived the situation. This creates the emotions you feel as well as the physical bodily sensations you feel (tensions, shaking, sweating etc). In the case of the spider, you would probably be feeling fear and the very familiar feeling of adrenaline coursing through your body.

        ii)   The second response is the 'what do I do' response – the RE-ACTION. This is where you do something to restore pleasure or avoid pain. This is where you physically flick the spider off and go running off screaming into the back yard.

A Parent's Guide To Balance *And Getting More 'You' Time.*

So what does all this have to do with time management?

It has everything to do with it because the reason you spend time doing what you do is due to the evaluation process occurring in your brain every minute of every day.

The reason you feel so stressed and anxious about your to do list is because you are evaluating it as a 'must do' list – things you "must do' in order to reach some expectation you have learnt to believe is probably going to make you worthy, valuable, successful or perceived by others as a 'good' person. The ultimate pursuit of emotional pleasure is a sense of worthiness.

Alas, you have just come across the incorrect thinking behind your stress about your time management. 'If I don't achieve xx, then I won't be worthy, or I will feel worth … less.'

If you want to learn how to stop becoming consumed by your busy life and to make the most out of your time, we need to first investigate your perceptions of your time and second, how you are evaluating the different options of how to spend your time.

This chapter's opening quote by Allison Mitchell makes a very valid point about time management. If you wish to create balance in your life, then before you even begin to try and manage your time, you need to understand the fundamentals of choice and focus.

A Parent's Guide To Balance *And Getting More 'You' Time.*

Why do I CHOOSE to FOCUS on what I do?

Every decision we make and action we take comes from our priorities *in each moment*. *"I choose to do this because it is a priority right now"*. Our priorities come from whatever beliefs are accessed by our brain during the evaluation process *in each moment*.

I emphasise the phrase, 'in each moment' because the brain is constantly receiving new information from our experiences and evaluating this information in accordance with the information accessed in the brain in that moment. This will influence the response you have to the current situation – what I feel and what I do about it right now.

For example, I have an intention to write this book, however there have been multiple moments just in the last five minutes where I have thought about what email might be in my inbox or what responses I might be getting to a Facebook post I wrote earlier. I keep getting distracted and have several times been very close to interrupting my writing to check.

Habitually my brain is looking for the instant gratification (the pleasure) of connecting with people and avoiding having to do more work (avoiding pain).

But then I consciously remind myself of another priority that brings my attention back on task. I have put myself on a deadline to finish this book by a certain time so I can move on to other things and launch my website in the required time. Doing this will mean I get to have more time for my family and bring in more income to the home, thus relieving some financial pressure.

Because the latter option is much more important to me than going on Facebook and checking my emails, I am continuing on with writing.

My priority in this moment was habitually to receive instant gratification and this is why we can often spend a lot of time getting distracted by things we ultimately wouldn't rate as being overly important. The brain is instinctively geared to pursue pleasure and avoid pain in every moment.

But with a little conscious reminder of the bigger picture goal, you can bring your focus back into alignment.

The bottom line is we make decisions based on what is the most important option to us, *in that moment.*

Our CHOICES come about as a result of what we FOCUS on and this is what you need to investigate if you wish to manage your time efficiently.

Our FOCUS is dependent upon whatever priority beliefs (the most important beliefs) have been activated by the brain in the process of evaluation.

Our choices are the end result, a REACTION (from the response part of the evaluation process) to how we've evaluated a situation and are an active attempt to restore or pursue pleasure and avoid pain.

A Parent's Guide To Balance *And Getting More 'You' Time.*

Spending loads of time just on traditional time management techniques and learning organisation skills may work in the short term, but in terms of eliminating stress in the long term, these methods will only work when life is going to plan and you are adhering to your schedule. When you don't stick to the plan, and life doesn't always go to plan, you will find yourself getting all stressed again.

This is because all you are doing is putting a band aid on the real problem. You are only fixing the symptoms, not the cause. The cause of your stress comes from how you have perceived the event (evaluated it) and what you believe it means about you (pleasure or pain).

That's why traditional time management techniques do not always mean the end of your stress.

Behind a busy stressed out person is a mindset attached to a belief about what they feel they 'must do' to get life right in order to feel good enough and worthy. That's what we need to change before managing our time.

The Mind TRACK to Happiness process

You will find in all of the products at the Parental Stress Centre we use a method I created called the Mind TRACK to Happiness process.

This process is a five step exercise using the acronym of the word TRACK to help you to remember each step.

A Parent's Guide To Balance *And Getting More 'You' Time.*

Here is what each step stands for:

T – Thoughts

R – Reality

A – Aim

C – Choices, options and solutions

K – Know your plan and action it.

Before we can change something that is causing us stress in our life we first need to understand the thinking behind the stress and re-align with the reality of the situation. This means taking a reality based approach to life. Only from the place of aligning to your reality, can you then focus on solutions for change.

All stress comes from a conflict between belief and reality. The belief is what I'm thinking about the event and what I think it means about me. The reality is what is actually happening and a realistic understanding of life and my self-worth.

Think of the five steps on the TRACK process as if you are climbing a ladder.

In the context of your time the bottom of the ladder is where things are in disarray in your life. You feel completely overwhelmed with all of your obligations, feel like nothing is getting done, as if you're disorganised and you need some good quality 'you' time.

A Parent's Guide To Balance *And Getting More 'You' Time.*

Before you get to the 'what do I do' stage, you must first climb the TRACK ladder to understand how you've gotten to where you are and why you are feeling so stressed about your reality.

Why your life is in disarray comes largely from how you have been evaluating life, so this is where we must begin.

Steps One and Two of the Mind TRACK to Happiness Process: Thoughts and Reality

Understanding the thinking behind your CHOICES and FOCUS

In theory, it may seem like an insurmountable task to have to sift through all of the thoughts causing your stress. After all we have around 60,000 thoughts a day!

However, it might surprise you to know all of these thoughts can be narrowed down and categorised into three viewpoints (or lenses) with one major belief at the core.

Remember all stress is a conflict between belief and reality, so these lenses are all in conflict with reality and need changing (upgrading).

Lens One – A Right vs a Wrong Life

This particular lens involves being attached to a particular picture of how you feel life is supposed to go.

A Parent's Guide To Balance *And Getting More 'You' Time.*

This might include:
- a clean house,
- the right way for your relationship to be,
- the right way for your children to behave,
- the right way for you to behave,
- the right way others are meant to treat you,
- the right way to achieve a goal.

Through this lens you have an expectation and you believe it has to go that way. This is where anxiety kicks in. Anxiety is all about control – "I feel like I have to control life so it goes right, and prevent anything from going wrong with my life".

Why?

"Because if life goes wrong, I believe it will mean something about the value of me and my life."

From your experiences over time you have learnt to attach the value of your life to getting life right and have adopted ideas on exactly how you think that's supposed to happen.

If life is not going to plan, you start to view life or the event as going wrong and start to feel bad. With anxiety, your need to control kicks in and you start to put more measures in place to further prevent your life from going wrong and get it to go right again.

A Parent's Guide To Balance *And Getting More 'You' Time.*

To a degree we all do this. For example, if it looks like it's going to rain we will take an umbrella so we don't get wet or we rearrange our plans for another day when it's not raining.

However with anxiety, there is an attachment, a desperation almost, for things to go right and meet your expected picture. It becomes something you must achieve, rather than something you want to achieve. You put lots of plans in place to prevent things from going wrong and even more plans in place just in case that goes wrong too. Anxiety can occur either mildly or to the point where it becomes extreme, obsessive or irrational.

With depression you go the other way. Because you've not been able to get life to go right, you start to feel like you are failing. You begin to feel like giving up on it all. It's just too hard. You're never going to get your life to go right. You're never going to be on top of things. You're never going to reach your goal, so what's the point. You stop setting goals and making plans either because of the fear of being a failure or because you already feel like one.

Depression and anxiety and how to overcome these illnesses are issues that are covered much more deeply in our *BE the Change* webinar series, so if you are identifying with what I'm saying here, you might want to check out this product.

The right vs wrong lens of life always centres round the idea there is a right way to live and a wrong way to live. If

I'm getting it right, then life is going well. If I'm getting it wrong, then life isn't going well (it's worth-less).

Lens Two – I am (my kids are) missing out

Once the brain starts to judge your life (or the event) as going wrong it then starts to look for the proof of this wrong life and starts to become aware of all the things you are missing out on.

- My kids aren't listening to me.
- I'm not getting any respect.
- No one cares what I do around here.
- This house is never clean.
- I'm never going to get any time out.
- I have no balance in my life.
- I don't know who I am anymore.

We enter into conversations about how bad life is and what we feel our life is missing, and what we would be getting if life was on the right path.

This type of thinking, again, is in conflict with the reality of what actually is happening. It's very hard to FOCUS on solutions when you all your attention is stuck on what is going wrong with your life and how much you are missing out on. There's not enough attention left to notice what is going right, and you can't see the forest for the trees.

Lens Three – I/they should have acted differently.

Now that life is not going right and you are missing out, the reasoning part of the brain kicks in and looks for why you are experiencing this situation in this way.

Now the focus gets shifted to who is to blame.

- I should have…
- They should have…
- Why didn't they…
- He could have made 'x' decisions.

Looking at things through this lens we start to become further in conflict with reality by thinking you or someone else should have acted differently.

These three lenses are the assumptions we draw about life, which all spiral down to the fundamental core belief that underlies all stress – my life is of less value.

Lens Four – Me or my life's value is of less value (worth-less).

What does 'this' mean about me?

This is the primary focus of the human brain's evaluation process. You are constantly rating whether something is good or bad, whether the event is causing pleasure or

A Parent's Guide To Balance *And Getting More 'You' Time.*

pain and establishing what this event means about you as a person and the value of your life.

As I mentioned before a sense of worthiness is the ultimate emotional pleasure and everyone wants to feel good, be accepted, approved of, loved and nurtured. With this instinctive agenda to receive pleasure in terms of our value, there is always a self-interest in the decisions we make and the actions we take.

Even when doing something charitable, there is still an agenda to feel good from seeing the pleasure of giving to others. We simply cannot escape this instinctual human desire.

The only reason you feel stress is because you have rated this 'wrong' event as meaning something about you and your life, that because you're missing out, your life's value has decreased. If you or they had just done something different then your life would be on that right path. You would be feeling good and life would be better.

Here's an example of how the four lenses play out in a time management situation causing stress:

Let's take a typical mother with three children trying to get out the door on time for school. She has accidentally slept in a full hour and she has to get lunches ready, two kids ready for school and one to day care and is attached to the belief she cannot walk out the door when the house is messy.

A Parent's Guide To Balance *And Getting More 'You' Time.*

Here's the mental monologue going on in her head:

"Oh no, I'm supposed to be up by now (right vs wrong – lens 1). I shouldn't have slept in. Why didn't I get up when my alarm went off? I know my mornings are chaotic. I should've just hauled my tired self out of bed (should/could – lens 3). Now I'm going to suffer all morning (missing out – lens 2). I'm such an idiot (my/my life's value decrease – lens 4)"

With her mindset already in conflict with reality, this mum is not seeing solutions. Her focus is stuck on what was supposed to happen and what's now not going to happen. By not readjusting her picture to the new reality and working out solutions from there, she is stuck in the stressful thinking mindset. She goes into anxiety mode because she's feeling out of control. She hasn't been able to stick to her routine to get the kids out the door on time like she normally does.

"I'm never going to make it on time. I don't have time to pack these lunches. I don't even know what I'm going to put in them (Missing out – lens 2). I should've gone shopping yesterday. Why can't these kids hurry up? They shouldn't be playing. They should be getting ready. Why aren't they listening to me (should/could – lens 3). This is not the way the morning is supposed to go. I need to be organised. I can't be getting up late and rushing around like this. It just doesn't work this way. How am I going to get this house cleaned in time? It's going to be a mess when I get home and I can't stand it when the house is messy (Right vs wrong – lens 1). I'm so useless. I'm lazy. I'm hopeless at

A Parent's Guide To Balance *And Getting More 'You' Time.*

this organisation thing. Other people are so much better at this motherhood thing than me. I never get things to go the way they should. I'm hopeless (Me/my life's value decrease – lens 4)"

Next time you are feeling stressed about your busy life try to take notice of your own internal monologue and see if you can identify the four viewpoints. They'll all be there and often one is more dominant than the other.

Remember, the cause of your stress is a conflict between belief and reality.

Step one of the Mind TRACK to happiness process is to recognise the thinking causing your stress. You can't change what you don't acknowledge.

If you're still wondering what all this has to do with your chaotic, unorganised, and busy life, then look further at your judgements. The words chaotic and unorganised are both judgements. They are judgements that come from your beliefs about how your life is different (wrong) from your right life.

"I'm supposed to have a chaotic free life. I'm supposed to be organised (Right vs wrong – lens 1). *Because it's not organised and doesn't run smoothly, I'm not enjoying my life* (missing out – lens2). *I should be able to change how my life runs. I shouldn't have to do so much all the time. I shouldn't be so busy* (should/could – lens 3). *I don't like my life when it's like this* (value decrease – lens 4)."

A Parent's Guide To Balance *And Getting More 'You' Time.*

The reality is you may have a busy life with a lot on your plate and this might be a reality you are not accepting right now. That conflict with reality is what is causing you stress. What you think this busy life means about you and your quality of life (your value) is what is causing your stress.

When stuck in these stressful lenses, your choices tend to become a desperate attempt to regain control of the situation. Irrational choices can be made that further complicate the situation and cause further stress. It's difficult to look at the situation with clarity – you're too focussed on how it's going wrong.

What is needed is an upgraded perspective on your life and the ability to be able to accept the reality of where you are right now. You don't have to like your reality, but you do need to accept it so you can free up your focus to move onto the solutions to help you change your reality.

Which brings us to step two of the Mind track to Happiness Process – Reality: the ability to upgrade your thinking.

Step Two of the Mind TRACK to Happiness Process: Reality

Upgrading your thinking to be in alignment with reality

When we talk about reality, I am addressing two aspects of reality – the reality of the situation and the reality of the bigger picture – how we all experience life.

A Parent's Guide To Balance *And Getting More 'You' Time.*

When you're looking at the reality of the situation, you need to accept how life really is. There's no denying it. The reality "is what it is". No amount of conversing and complaining about how it shouldn't be like it is will change that.

If your life is busy somehow it was created that way. It's irrelevant to dwell on how and why – reality is life is now busy.

From the place of accepting the reality of the situation, you now need to work on your perception of what this reality means, because how you are perceiving your busy life is what is actually causing your stress, not the fact that you have a busy life.

Question: Do all people who have a busy life feel stressed?

Answer: No. This is because they have a different viewpoint on what that busy life means. If it was your busy life that caused stress then everyone who was busy would feel stressed. But that's simply not the case.

Upgrading the four stressful thinking lenses

For each of the four stressful thinking lenses, there is a matching upgrade to help you to easily change the way you are perceiving things.

A Parent's Guide To Balance *And Getting More 'You' Time.*

Stressful thinking lens #1: Right vs Wrong Life
Reality Based Upgrade #1: Life is a story of ups and downs

When we are stressed we have become attached to the idea of the right way life was supposed to unfold and are in conflict with the reality of how it actually is unfolding.

Over time we have been indoctrinated to believe life should go in this straight line towards your goal, but that expectation is in conflict with reality.

The reality is life is a story of ups and downs. Sometimes we get what we want and sometimes we don't. Some events are expected, some are not. Sometimes you enjoy experiences, other times you won't. Sometimes you feel organised and sometimes you are not.

Logically we know life doesn't always go to plan, yet we still get stressed when it doesn't. This is because logic is not what is driving your mindset. Logic is a conscious aspect of the brain, whereas habits (and thus habitual thinking) happen on an unconscious level.

With awareness you can start to recognise this stressful thinking and consciously start to change that thinking. Over time, with repetition and consistently applying these upgrades, you will reprogram the subconscious to habitually think in a reality-based way. But it has to be done using conscious effort first.

A Parent's Guide To Balance *And Getting More 'You' Time.*

Whenever you notice yourself getting attached to the expectations you had for how your day, week or life was supposed to play out, you need to remind yourself that life doesn't always go this way and it is okay. You're not here to get life right all the time and the reality is no one ever does.

If your life is going wrong when life doesn't go to plan, then everyone's life is wrong because no one lives on a straight path to their desires. We all experience ups and downs and all of those experiences make up our life's unique story. It shapes us and makes us who we are and all of our events are linked. All of our highs ultimately lead to our lows and vice versa.

If you were to entertain the fantasy that you could turn back time and undo the previous events leading to this current unwanted reality, you would have to get in your little time machine and undo every single experience linked to that decision – the beliefs behind your decisions and every single event contributing to the creation of those beliefs. Then you would have to go back and undo the decisions and the beliefs for everyone else who played a role in your development. It's likely you would be gone a very long time.

The reality is all of your events just lead to another experience and ALL of your experiences have led you to where you are right now. There is never just one event responsible for what you are currently experiencing. There is always a long line of experiences, lessons, decisions and actions that led to it.

A Parent's Guide To Balance *And Getting More 'You' Time.*

Bottom line – reality is whatever is happening right now. It's not a reflection of a right or wrong life. It's simply a part of the experiences you are having in life. It doesn't mean anything about you.

This upgrade is about being able to accept whatever is happening in your life right now and see it as part of your life's story, not a definition of its success.

Stressful thinking lens #2: Missing out
Reality Based Upgrade #2: Everything has value

Have you ever experienced something that at the time you judged as being wrong, yet it taught you a really important lesson you wouldn't take back for the world?

This is happening all the time, in every moment, we just don't focus on it. We're too busy rolling around in what we don't have and what we are missing out on.

In amongst this chaotic life where the kids are running amok, the house is a pigsty, nothing is going the way you want and you are feeling incredibly worn out, there is immense value.

Your children are learning what to do (often by learning what NOT to do). You are learning you can't always have a clean house and how to let go of the attachment to needing it to be that way. Perhaps you are learning how to be more organised. Let's face it, you wouldn't even be reading this book if you had not experienced stress in your life and thus wouldn't be learning what you are.

A Parent's Guide To Balance *And Getting More 'You' Time.*

Your experiences are always teaching you something and adding knowledge to your life. You are constantly receiving event learning where you are learning how to do something or do it better, or you are getting life learning, how to understand your experiences in the context of the bigger picture. For example, life doesn't always go to plan and my life is not worth-less if it doesn't meet my expectation.

Even though you aren't getting what you want you are always getting what you need in order to grow as a human being. Are you the same person you were 10 years ago? No. You have loads more knowledge and experience. This came from ALL of your experiences – the highs and the lows.

Rather than focus on what you are missing out on, shift your focus on what you are getting. Find the hidden good in the bad. Look for evidence of the lessons you are learning or your children are learning for their development. Look for how this unwanted experience is leading you towards some other wanted experience. Look for how your current reality is giving you a wakeup call – you need to make changes and learn how to do something differently in order to live a more enjoyable life.

These unwanted events are a gift to you just as much as achieving our goals and desires are. How do I know what to do or even what I want until I've experienced what not to do or what I don't want?

A Parent's Guide To Balance *And Getting More 'You' Time.*

This doesn't mean you should accept it and do nothing about it. It just means you are accepting the reality of what is happening in your life right now, you understand it couldn't have happened any other way because of how everything has unfolded before this moment. Your life today is contributing to the knowledge and experience that will contribute to the experiences you have tomorrow.

When you accept the reality of what is happening in your life, stop seeing it as wrong and start seeing it as part of the ups and downs of life, and you can find value in it, your focus is no longer in conflict with reality.

<u>Stressful thinking lens #3:</u> I/they should have acted differently
<u>Reality Based Upgrade #3:</u> Priority beliefs dictate behaviour (in any given moment)

This upgrade will help you to eliminate blame towards yourself and towards others for how your life is playing out.

Let's think about how the brain evaluates life again. It experiences the world with the five senses and evaluates the information received from the senses in accordance with the data already stored in the brain.

It evaluates what this situation means and what it says about you. It is focussed on pursuing pleasure and avoiding pain and with this in mind, a priority belief about what it means and what you should do and feel about the situation (the response) is selected.

A Parent's Guide To Balance *And Getting More 'You' Time.*

Whichever belief is selected will be the belief your brain rated as being most important in that moment. That is, the belief which was going to give you the most pleasure or prevent the most pain.

Let's take for example the two options to get out of bed on time or go back to sleep for that extra few minutes (which turned into an hour).

You might be rolling around in the belief you shouldn't have stayed in bed, however you are in conflict with the reality of why you did it in the first place.

When faced with the obnoxious little beeping sound waking you from your slumber, your brain went into evaluation mode and very quickly established what the sound was and what it meant about you. It means you have to get up now. But you don't want to. You just got to sleep after a restless night and want to keep sleeping (pleasure). The other side of the argument is saying you have to get up so you will be organised and won't experience a chaotic, crazy morning where everyone's running late and there are meltdowns going on left, right and centre.

Which option wins?

Well that depends on which one is rated as being the most important *in that moment*. Whichever one was rated as giving you the most pleasure (or deemed to increase your quality of life) in that moment will always win out. We are always making decisions with our best interests at heart.

A Parent's Guide To Balance *And Getting More 'You' Time.*

However, once you make that decision and experience the consequences you are given new information that can sometimes make you believe you should have made a different decision in the past. But you didn't have that information then, or it wasn't strong enough information in that moment to sway your decision. It's only now you are experiencing the pain that you think you should have made a different decision.

To harp on about how you should've done something differently is in conflict with the reality that *in the moment* of making the decision your brain assessed all of the information it had and accessed a stronger belief that resulted in you taking the particular action you did. It couldn't have been any other way.

We don't control which beliefs our subconscious mind habitually chooses, but with awareness of that thinking and the knowledge to upgrade it, which is what you are getting in this book, you can consciously change those thoughts once they have arisen.

In terms of what other people should have done, the same theory applies. Their brains are working in the same way. They are accessing the information they have and determining decisions and actions based on their priority beliefs – that is which belief is the strongest and holds the most importance for getting what they want (pleasure) and avoiding pain.

A Parent's Guide To Balance *And Getting More 'You' Time.*

If you want to change a person's behaviour, you have to change how they evaluate life. This is actually the core teachings behind our *Stress Free Parenting* webinar series. We spend so much time on using traditional disciplinary methods, like time out, however if we spent more time learning how to understand our child's evaluation system and change it, we wouldn't have to deal with so much of the 'bad' behaviour in our children to begin with. If you want more information on this webinar series, check out the products page on our website to learn more.

For now with this upgrade, we must realise we make decisions based on the information we hold in that moment and the priority beliefs accessed. Why we do what we do is because of how we think.

Our children don't listen because it's not a priority in that moment for them to listen. I bet if you said it again with the tagline 'If you don't do this, you lose your video games for a week' you'll find their priority suddenly changes.

Equally so, if you were to say "If you do 'x' we'll go to your favourite theme park today' you also may get them to shift their priorities. It's all about understanding how the other person is evaluating the situation and using it to negotiate and compromise – you get what you want, while they get what they want.

In the context of time, you are choosing where and how to invest your energy with the current beliefs you have and which ones hold the most importance *in each moment.*

A Parent's Guide To Balance *And Getting More 'You' Time.*

Behind each choice will be a 'what's in it for me' story. There is always something you get out of spending the time where you do.

That's why time management is not about time, it's about choice and focus. Where I put my focus is how I make my choices and sometimes this focus is coming from deeply ingrained habits of thinking that have come from years of conditioning.

Whatever has happened that was different to your expectations, it is pointless to lay blame on anybody and get caught up in should've/could've talk, because all that is doing is keeping more of your focus in conflict with reality and less on dealing with your new reality.

So accept that reality, forgive and move on. To do this though, you may need to understand the final upgrade….

Stressful thinking lens #4: Me/my life has decreased in value
Reality Based Upgrade 4#: My life is always valuable

Okay, so this one can be a toughie to get your head around because we are so heavily conditioned to believe our worth is conditional. It's ingrained in us since we were born and were exposed to the 'do this and you'll get this' concept.

Society thrives on promoting the conditions of our worth. Buy this product so your life can be better (worth more). Don't miss out on this opportunity or you'll be sorry (life

A Parent's Guide To Balance *And Getting More 'You' Time.*

will be worth-less). You'd better comply with society's rules or you won't be liked (you'll be rated as worth-less).

There are rules about morals, education, status, religion and cultural standards, and many more, that we learn to live by, all with the connotation that meeting these 'rules' will earn you a valuable place in society and your life will be rated as worthy.

This constant conditioning combined with our naturally evaluating and judging brain, means we will always rate ourselves as being worth more or worth less and that's not likely to change.

What we can change is to recognise the incorrectness of this rating by being aware of the bigger picture of the true value of your life – knowing your true self-worth.

Consider this question for a moment:

Who takes the credit for there being bread in your home?

Whenever I ask this question, the first answer I usually get is, me. I buy it. Fair enough. Who else? How did it get there?

The baker made it. So does he get the credit? Or is it the person who makes the ingredients of the bread? Or is it the person who delivers those ingredients to the store that makes the bread? Is it the person at the checkout that sold you the bread, or the owner of the store that allows you to be able to buy the bread? Does the wheat harvester take credit for the bread, or is it the person who invented the

A Parent's Guide To Balance *And Getting More 'You' Time.*

machinery used to harvest the wheat to make the bread? Or is the parents who gave birth to everyone involved with the bread making? Or is it their parents who gave birth to them, who gave birth to the bread makers?

You get my point. If you go back far enough, everyone would be able to take some credit for bread being in your home, because everyone played an important role in its creation.

Think about who you are right now as a person. Think about what you've learnt – physically, mentally and emotionally. Think about the achievements you have had and the mistakes you have made. Who takes the credit for you being who you are today? Is it just you? Or are there thousands of people that you can credit for you learning everything you have learnt to date?

Also, were all of those things learnt because life went to plan, or was it because life sometimes didn't go to plan as well?

The reality is every experience you've had in your life has contributed to who you are today and thousands of people have played valuable roles in the making of you.

Guess what? You are doing that for other people's lives too. Just by being you, you are already important to the world because you are contributing the knowledge you have and the experiences you are having with the people around you.

A Parent's Guide To Balance *And Getting More 'You' Time.*

They learn from you, get information from you and have experiences with you that contribute to the decisions they make and the actions they take and hence how their lives unfold. They couldn't have had those experiences without you or without the thousands of other people they came in contact with.

Using the information and lessons they received from you they then influence the people around them and influence how their lives unfold. You've just become an important part of their lives too.

The reason your life is ALWAYS valuable is because of your very existence.

Self-worth has nothing to do with what you know, what you do, the house being clean or dirty, whether you get life right, achieve what you want, or any other expectation you are attaching your worth to. You are worthy right now just by being you.

Understanding this perspective you can now let go of what you 'have' to achieve in order to make life valuable and you can now start to focus on what you 'want' to experience in your life.

Applying the upgrades

When you apply all four reality thinking upgrades you will find yourself able to deal with the busyness of your days a lot more easily.

A Parent's Guide To Balance *And Getting More 'You' Time.*

You become aligned with the reality "it is okay that life doesn't always go to plan". You're able to recognise and let go of your attachments to your 'to do' list and do what you can.

When life doesn't go to plan you start to look for the hidden good and how this experience is actually providing you (or your children) with valuable information to help you to learn.

You become more understanding of other people's behaviour. You won't necessarily like all of their behaviour, but you will recognise their behaviour is not about you, it's all about them and how they have perceived their lives.

When you are interacting with your children you start to see their behaviour as being an indication of what you still need to teach them or how you need to alter their perception of life. You don't take their behaviour so personally and you become more solution focussed about teaching them what they need to know so their behaviour will change.

And finally, you start to become more at peace with your life and see your current life as just a launching pad for you to build the life you want. You start to be able to accept all the different ups and downs of your life because you no longer *need* life to go to plan to understand your value.

You'll still try to get what you want, we'll never stop doing that, but you will no longer see your 'to do' list as a 'must-do-or-it-means-something-bad-about-me-and-my-life' list.

A Parent's Guide To Balance *And Getting More 'You' Time.*

From here you create the space in your focus to start looking for solutions on how to get the life you want to experience.

Which brings us to the next step of the Mind TRACK to Happiness Process – Aim.

Step Three of the Mind TRACK to Happiness Process: Aim

What do I want?

Now we start getting to the more practical part of managing your time. It's probably what you initially thought you were signing up for, but you're now going to be able to look at this step with a lot more clarity and realism than before.

You are no longer *needing* life to be right in order to know it's valuable and you are now more able to accept the ups and downs of life without stress, because you are now aware of its value and the inevitable truth that it will just lead to another experience.

Or at least you have the knowledge to keep practicing this way of thinking, because it all takes time and practice.

Before you start looking at what you want to do with your time and how you'd like to manage it, there a couple of investigative steps we need to take to figure out what you actually are doing with your time and the discrepancies between what you want and what you are presently doing.

A Parent's Guide To Balance *And Getting More 'You' Time.*

Exercise One: What do I do with My Time?

Ever say things like "where did the time go?", "I don't know what I did today", "gee, is it that time already?", or "I haven't achieved anything on my list today".

This is what often happens when we are not deliberate about our time, or when we get caught up in some mindless activity that is far from what we had intended to do. That is when our priority in the moment became about instant gratification rather than our longer term aim.

This exercise is designed to help you to get real about what you do with your time. You might be surprised from this exercise alone just how much time you are spending on activities you don't even rate as being that important.

Step One

Use this form for at least three days and list in as much detail as possible what you do in each hour.

Morning

Time of Day	What did you do	Step Two
5.00 – 6.00am		
6.00 – 7.00am		

A Parent's Guide To Balance *And Getting More 'You' Time.*

7.00 – 8.00am		
8.00 – 9.00am		
9.00 – 10.00am		
10.00 – 11.00am		
11.00 – 12.00pm		

Afternoon

Time of Day	What did you do	Step Two
12.00 – 1.00pm		
1.00 – 2.00pm		
2.00 – 3.00pm		
3.00 – 4.00pm		
4.00 – 5.00pm		
5.00 – 6.00pm		

www.ParentalStress.com.au

A Parent's Guide To Balance *And Getting More 'You' Time.*

Evening

6.00 – 7.00pm		
7.00 – 8.00pm		
8.00 – 9.00pm		
9.00 – 10.00pm		
10.00 – 11.00pm		
11pm onwards		
After 11pm		

Step Two

After you have filled in your time sheet, go back and reflect on the activities you have engaged in over that period. Write beside your activities whether you consider the activity to be:

    a. Highly important to you

    b. Medium importance

    c. Low importance

    d. An outright waste of time

A Parent's Guide To Balance *And Getting More 'You' Time.*

What is really important to me?

We have learnt the reality of how choices are made comes from what we have deemed to be important to us *in each moment*.

However, when you reflect on the activities you actually engage in, you might find the reality of what you do tells a different story.

Often what we think is important to us, or what we want to hold as important, wasn't actually where we ultimately ended up spending our time.

For example, you may believe it is important to spend quality time with your children and, if asked, you might say this is one of the most important values you have as a parent. However, the reality might be you more often than not tell your child you don't have time to play with them because of some other household chore or errand you have to do.

Or you might find yourself doing something on the computer or reading a magazine instead of spending time with your children.

Your priority in the moment wasn't spending time with your child, it was about something else – what you were going to get out of the other activity became the priority over the value of spending time with your child.

This isn't a judgment on your character. Let's not go down the 'I'm not good enough' road. There is no right or wrong here. What we are doing is simply gaining insight into our

A Parent's Guide To Balance *And Getting More 'You' Time.*

habitual evaluation system when it comes to where you are spending your time.

All we are doing at this point of the book is establishing an understanding of how your beliefs are contributing to your lack of time management and why you aren't able to get things to function smoothly in your home.

Exercise Two: What's important to me?

Step One

Reflect on exercise one where you have taken notice of where you have spent your time.

Write down all the things you did on that list that you rated as being highly important or of medium importance and why you list those things as being important and what is in it for you (remember, there will always be something in it for you. After all, that's why you rated it as important).

For example, work might have taken up a fair bit of your time and you may have rated that as being highly important. Why? What's the story behind that rating? Do you need to bring income into my family? The benefit to you is you are living up to your moral belief of being a responsible parent and perhaps you also get a more comfortable lifestyle out of it too?

Highly important activities

_____
_____
_____

A Parent's Guide To Balance *And Getting More 'You' Time.*

Why is this activity important?

_____
_____
_____

What is in it for me?

_____
_____
_____

Step Two

Was there anything on your schedule you haven't listed that you would rate as being highly important or of medium importance?

Make a list of these too below.

Highly important activities

_____
_____
_____

Why is this activity important?

_____
_____
_____

What is in it for me?

_____
_____
_____

A Parent's Guide To Balance *And Getting More 'You' Time.*

Step Three

Take a look at your schedule again and now look at the things you did that you rated as least important. Think about why that activity was important to you in that moment and what was in it for you. This will help you to get insight as to why you get distracted by those activities instead of doing the things you do rate as being important.

Least important activities

_____
_____
_____

Why was this activity important

_____
_____
_____

What is in it for me?

_____
_____
_____

** Important note **

You might be tempted to skip these parts, but please bear with the process. We are building on getting to the part where you are creating a clear plan of action to bring your life more balance and freedom from guilt. You will soon know you are doing exactly what you want to be doing, as well as attending to the areas you hold of great importance.

These steps are integral parts of your ability to establish this plan.

Getting Organised

Okay, now we start to get really solution focussed.

Before you began reading this book I suspect a lot of your focus was looking through the missing out lens and thinking about how you never get anything done, life is too chaotic, there's never enough time for you, or you can't get this done because of that, etc.

While you are investing your energies in this kind of talk how much attention does that leave for looking at what you do want and how to get it?

This is what we are moving onto now.

How do I *want* to spend my time?

Before you begin creating a time schedule that will incorporate everything you hold important and all the other things you need to do, your first step is to establish how you *want* to schedule your time.

This is the whole point of the AIM step on the TRACK process – shifting your focus away from stressful thinking, accepting the reality of the present moment and focussing on what you do want. The final two steps of the process are the how to get it and the plan itself.

Consider the following six categories, and how much time you would like to put into each category in general.

Time-out just for me

This is time where you get to do something for yourself, whether it is reading a book, participating in sport, watching a movie, seeing friends, or whatever. This category is about doing what you want to do. On page 73 we extensively discuss this topic of taking 'me' time, as I know as parents we often let this one slip by the wayside believing it's not as important as other things. In part B of this book, we help you to allow yourself to schedule this much needed time in – guilt free.

Quality Time with the Kids

This category is about spending some one on one time with the children, either individually or collectively, or both. There is no running off to put clothes on the line or doing the dishes, this time is exclusively for you to have fun and connect with each other.

Quality Time with my partner

This category keeps you connected with your partner. Whether you are just talking about your day, planning your future, or even a night away from the kids, you need to get specific about how much time and how often you want to spend time in this area.

Doing the housework or running errands

This category is where you can list all of the things you need to complete in a week, such as housework and running errands, taking kids to sports and appointments, etc. You can also list how much time in a week you will spend doing these things.

Work

How much time does work take up of your life? If you have flexible hours, you might note how much time you would like to allocate to work. If you don't have flexible hours, just make note of how much time you do spend working so that you can factor it in to your schedule.

Miscellaneous

This category is for all of the miscellaneous items that come up – unusual appointments (doctors, bank etc.) or regular items in your life that we've not included above.

A note on the household chores and running errands category.

It's worth noting this category may be the one that makes us feel the most unbalanced in our lives. You may feel as

A Parent's Guide To Balance *And Getting More 'You' Time.*

if there are so many things you need to do and seemingly not enough time, so you often get stressed about how to manage it all.

The first step when trying to achieve all of the household chores and errands is to get them out of your head and onto paper.

Part of the stress you experience comes from your brain trying to remember everything, prioritise it and perform it in a clear and balanced way. There is so much to think about you tend to get into brain overload and feel overwhelmed and unorganised.

For example, let's say you are trying to get the kids ready for day care or school and get organised for your day. While they are at day care you have a doctor appointment to show him some X-rays, you have an appointment with the bank manager to go over a loan and you need to go grocery shopping. In order to do all of these things there are many things you need to do to prepare yourself.

If you tried to organise all of this in your head this is what you would have to remember all at once:

- Get school lunches ready – Morning tea, afternoon tea, lunch and drinks. What healthy food do I get ready?
- Pack the school bags – spare clothes, nappies, wipes, hat, sunscreen, sleep sheets and blanket;
- Make breakfast;

A Parent's Guide To Balance *And Getting More 'You' Time.*

- Dress the kids;
- Brush their teeth;
- Brush their hair;
- Remember to take the X-rays with you;
- The bank manager needs a list of things for the meeting too:
    - proof of income,
    - tax returns,
    - proof of identification,
    - quotation for the item you are buying.
- Grocery shopping – you need milk, eggs, breakfast cereal, bread, biscuits, meat, pumpkin, potatoes … etc.

If you don't write all these things down, not only do you have to remember each and every point, but you also have to try and prioritise this list and carry it out without forgetting any of it. I haven't even mentioned any of the clothes washing, dishes or cleaning up that may take place during this morning of preparation.

Throw into the mix a cranky, clingy child or a tantrum from one (or more) of your children and you have the recipe for a disastrous, stressful morning.

You cannot possibly remember everything you need to do, prioritise everything correctly, handle unexpected interruptions and complete each task effectively without getting stressed and flustered, unless you write it down. Take the information out of your head and get it onto paper where you can see it, rearrange it where necessary and prioritise it more effectively.

Making Lists

The trick to organising your regular tasks, such as the household chores and errands, is to get into the habit of creating lists. In the next step you will create as many lists as you need to incorporate all of the regular things you need to do. Keep these lists nearby and check them off as you go through your day and your week. When we get to creating your schedule you can incorporate your lists into your schedule, so you include everything that needs doing.

If this is not clear, don't worry, it will become clearer as we continue, but for now, start by creating your own list, using the example as your guide:

Daily Housework

- 1 Load of washing per day
- Cook dinner
- Put washing on the clothes line
- Make the beds
- Fold washing and put it away

A Parent's Guide To Balance *And Getting More 'You' Time.*

- General tidy up and sweep
- Wash dishes – breakfast, lunch, dinner and snacks

Weekly Housework

- Change sheets on all beds
- Clean toilet and bathroom
- Mop floors
- Dust and polish furniture
- Clean glass doors
- Wipe fingerprints off doors and walls

Monthly Housework or other long-term house chores

- Vacuum floors
- Clean windows
- Sort kid's old clothes
- De-clutter cupboards
- Clean up outside
- Clean carpets
- Clean cupboards
- Clean the stove
- Clean the fridge

Day Care Preparation

- Kids' breakfasts
- Clean their teeth
- Get dressed and brush hair
- Make lunches and drinks
- Pack bag – with sleep sheets, hat, sun cream, nappies, wipes, lunch and drinks

These are just an example of some of the lists you may like to create to remind you of all the things you need to do within one task, or of all of the things you would like to achieve in a specified time, eg daily/weekly/monthly household chores.

Exercise Three – Making lists

Because there are so many things to think about within the area of housework/errands, to help you get clear about what's involved in this area, create your own lists according to your circumstances. This will help you both in day to day life, but also when it comes time to create your schedule later in step four of the TRACK process – choices.

If any of the other categories require detailed lists (for example a miscellaneous commitment that requires planning and time allocation, or work) create your daily, weekly and monthly lists for those categories too.

A Parent's Guide To Balance *And Getting More 'You' Time.*

Once you have done this you will have a better idea of how much time you need to allocate to the area of housework and errands to make you feel balanced in this area of your life.

Take notice as you do the next exercise of how much time you are allocating to each area and think about why it is your priority to add this much time to each item. Is your thinking in conflict with reality? Are you allocating that much time to prove something about yourself? Or is it just what you would like to experience to have life go as smoothly as possible?

Also, don't be afraid to think outside the square and consider your ideal situation, especially in areas where you are committed to activities you don't like or don't align with what you consider to be important. What would be the ideal of that situation?

While you may not be able to change those circumstances right now, having a specific ideal of how you would like it to be can get the cogs turning in the choices step. Here you will research HOW you can get this aim to come to life.

The AIM step is all about finding clarity in what you want to have happen in your life and making sure it is not coming from a worth-less belief, but from a place of simply wanting to experience a certain reality.

A Parent's Guide To Balance *And Getting More 'You' Time.*

Exercise Four – Establishing what I want

For each of the six categories listed above, allocate how much time it would take for you to feel balanced in each area of your life. You decide whether to do it in days, weeks or months, it just needs to be what you are happy with.

Don't worry at this point whether you will be able to spend that much time on each category, we will get to that later. For now just list what you would consider as acceptable for you to feel like your life was balanced and every area was getting adequate attention.

For example, this exercise might look like this:

Time out for me:

- At least 4 hours by myself per week.

Quality time with the kids:

- At least 1 hour per day of individual time with each child.
- At least 1 hour per day of combined time with all children.

Quality time with my husband:

- At least ½ hour per day of conversation and at least 1-2 hours a week of uninterrupted time together. One day or night out a month away from the kids, just for us.

A Parent's Guide To Balance *And Getting More 'You' Time.*

Doing the housework or running errands:

- About 2 hours a day of housework, which includes my weekly cleaning, general day to day tidying, washing and folding clothes, grocery shopping, etc.

Work:

- 8 hours per day on Mondays and Thursdays.

Miscellaneous:

- I will just rearrange my schedule to fit these items in when required.

Step Four of the Mind TRACK to Happiness Process: Choices

What are the choices, options and solutions available to get what I want.

So far we have established that time management is about choice and focus. We have explored what you consider is important to you, and you have decided how much time you would like to spend on each area of your life. With the lists you just created the next step is to do some research into how you can achieve everything on these lists.

For some of you it may just be a simple exercise of planning and scheduling your time accordingly because there's nothing different on your list to your normal everyday life, you just need to organise it more efficiently.

A Parent's Guide To Balance *And Getting More 'You' Time.*

For others, however, your ideal – what you want – might require some further investigation and research.

The choices step of the TRACK process is about finding the resources you need to get what you want.

For example, if your ideal scenario is to cut work back to part-time so you can be there more for the kids and have more you time, you will need to research how you're going to do this.

Ask yourself some questions:

- Who else is doing what I want to do?
- Where can I find the information to teach me how to do what I want to do?
- What resources, options and solutions are available to me that will get me what I want?

No one is ever stuck in a situation they can't get out of. If you are experiencing something you don't like it just means you don't yet have the information to get what you want, or there hasn't been enough time or action put in place to move on.

Rather than get stuck in your missing out lens again this step gets you to be solution focussed. Now that you have specific aims in place for what you want you need to sort out how you're going to get it.

This may be investigating what you may need to study to get a different job, or how to work from home. It may be investigating what other people are doing to get more time out, or looking into how to get more support with looking after your kids if you have no family and friends around to help you. What services are available to you that can help you get your aim?

There is always someone who has been in your position and has found a way out. There is always someone who has information you don't yet know that teaches you something to help you get what you want.

You just need to look for it.

Now you have the ability to upgrade your incorrect thinking to a reality based mindset you are able to accept the reality of the situation you are in. You've now set your aim, now you just have to FOCUS on how to get it.

Can you see how your mindset about time has completely shifted? The reality is nothing changes unless something changes. The first thing that needs to change in order for you to get the life you want is your mindset.

Get out of the 'woe is me, I don't have' line of thinking, accept your reality, establish what you want and do the research to figure out how to get it.

Exercise Five – How do I get what I want?

Take a look at the results of exercise four. What areas are not possible right now? What areas of your current

A Parent's Guide To Balance *And Getting More 'You' Time.*

life don't match your ideal of how you'd like it to be and require further investigation?

Isolate those areas and put your detective hat on. Research using the internet, government services, ask other mums and dads and seek out the information you need to get what you want.

Find the pathway you need to follow to get you the aim that you want.

This exercise may take some time, so don't give up if you don't find your answers straight away.

Remember, we find what we put our attention on, so if you really want something, keep looking and the answer will appear soon enough.

You will be using this information as we move into the fifth step of the Mind TRACK to Happiness Process – Know your plan and action it.

Step Five of the Mind TRACK to Happiness Process: Know your plan and action it

Create an action plan for a balanced life

This step is about bringing everything we've been working on into an actionable plan.

Having a plan of action is really valuable when you have a busy life. If you follow that plan as closely as possible you will experience the life you want to lead, because you have deliberately created it.

A Parent's Guide To Balance *And Getting More 'You' Time.*

This step is really reining in your FOCUS to be on what you hold important. It will give you the clarity and peace of mind you need because you will know all areas of your life are being attended to in the way you WANT. If they aren't quite there because what you want will take time, there will be comfort in the knowledge you have a clear pathway for how to get there.

This is going to free up so much of your energy because you are no longer stressing about not getting things done.

However, there are a few things to keep in mind as you go into creating your schedule.

Life doesn't always go to plan

Life is a story of ups and downs. This is reality. This plan you are about to create is a guide. Children will throw a spanner in the mix. You won't get out of bed in time sometimes. Other unexpected circumstances will pop up. Instant gratification and the allure of social media may suck you in and sway you from your plan.

It is important you don't get too emotionally attached to your plan or you will likely go back into stress again when you can't tick your boxes on your list.

If you do have something come up, accept reality, move on and reschedule. It's not the end of the world (and it's not the end of your self-worth either). It's just a reality of life.

A Parent's Guide To Balance *And Getting More 'You' Time.*

Always be aware of your thinking

Awareness is 50 percent of change. Stay aware of the thinking behind your choices and what beliefs are driving them. Keep the list of upgrades to those stressful thinking lenses handy to help keep you aligned with what is really important and what is 'real' in your life.

1. Ups and downs,
2. Value in everything,
3. Priority beliefs dictate yours/others behaviour in each moment, and
4. You are ALWAYS worthy.

Keep these truths firmly cemented in your mind and your life will be calmer and more peaceful (and your kids will learn that too).

In regards to the practical aspect of your schedule, you might want to keep these pointers in mind too.

Get organised before the day

If you schedule to do things when the kids are in bed, or at a time when you can allow more time to do them, it will help you to stay on schedule and reduce stress. If your children go to day care, or you have some appointment the next day that you need to prepare documents for, it seems more feasible to schedule this preparation at a time when you will be able to think clearly. Mornings can be chaotic, especially when unexpected events happen like a wet bed or unco-operative children. Doing these things the night before frees up more of your morning to attend to these unexpected events.

Meal Planning

Planning what you are going to cook for the week and making a shopping list for those meals can reduce the amount of time you spend standing in front of the fridge or cupboard trying to decide what to cook. If you organise your meals ahead of time you can factor in dietary requirements and taste at your leisure rather than on the spot when you only have half an hour to cook your meal. You will also be organised and have what you need in the fridge, so you won't need to quickly rush to the shops for a missing ingredient.

Delegate Responsibility

You don't have to do everything. Get the kids involved with the tidying up, get them into the routine of making their beds if they can, picking up their toys (even a two year old can do that) – a lot of the time at young ages, they love to do these things, especially if you make it fun.

Ask your partner to contribute more to the household running. Negotiate the fairness of what each of you do and see if there is room for delegating some of your tasks to him/her. You can learn more about how to communicate this with your partner in the relationships section of our website.

Also, if you are lacking in extra time, perhaps an option may be to ask for a friend or family member to help you out

A Parent's Guide To Balance *And Getting More 'You' Time.*

with the kids on occasion or consider putting them in day care for a day if they aren't already.

Perhaps there are government or community services that can help you with some of the things on your list. This is where the choices step comes in. Research it. You never know what you'll find.

Taking on everything yourself and not enlisting on some outside help is going to greatly hinder how much time you have for yourself and other activities.

If you do tend to take everything on yourself, you might want to go back to the thoughts and reality steps of the TRACK process. Try to identify why you do that and how to upgrade this thinking. There is likely to be a belief you are holding about why you should do everything yourself.

Your Family Dynamics

Create your schedule to align with the family dynamic you contribute to. If you have agreed that your partner works and you look after the kids and the housework that is the commitment you must honour, or deliberately renegotiate the agreement.

Whether it is spoken or assumed, the role you play in the family and the roles other members of the family play have been decided. This is reality. If you've changed your mind about how you want the roles to be within the home you can't just expect they will know that. You have to communicate your new wants and needs and reach a new alignment.

Whatever you want to do, it must align with family dynamics. It doesn't mean they will like the change, especially if you are always giving, giving, giving and all of a sudden you tell them you are going to take some time out.

However, because you have specifically spoken of the change they are not left confused about why you have suddenly stopped doing what they consider to be normal.

Do you need to add an extra time category from Step Three – AIM?

From the research you've done in step four of the TRACK process it may be necessary to add an additional time category into your scheduling to allow you to work on your aim.

For example, if you decided to get a more balanced work/family life you would need to take on more study you will need to add a study category into your schedule and allocate time to that. Or if you decided you want to work from home and have found a business that fits with your wants, but you still need to work while you are building that business, you will need to allocate extra time to building that business in amongst all your other commitments.

If you don't add this important category in it won't get done and you will begin to feel like you are not reaching your ideal. Your missing out lens will kick in again, leading you towards stress.

A Parent's Guide To Balance *And Getting More 'You' Time.*

This is where you may need to become flexible and weigh up the importance of each activity. The reality may be that the time you had allocated may not be possible when weighed up against all of the other categories.

Be conscious of your thinking when doing this exercise, because there will have to be some give and take. There are only so many hours in a day.

Remember the tips above for using the stressful thinking vs reality based thinking models to help you to know which areas to compromise on, or maybe even eliminate altogether.

At the end of the day, the whole objective of the plan is to make you feel like you are approaching all of the different demands in your life with a balance that you are happy with.

This may change over time, so don't be afraid to revisit your plan regularly.

Following is a personal example of three plans I created when I was a part-time stay at home mum of my two boys (then one and two years old), worked three days a week and was trying to establish my parenting coaching business from scratch.

This is a perfect example of working towards creating my aim of working for myself with completely flexible hours so I could be there for my children during their school years, which I'd always wanted to do as a parent.

A Parent's Guide To Balance *And Getting More 'You' Time.*

As a side note, it may seem like 5am is a particularly early time to get up, however, I was not blessed with children who liked to sleep in. Thankfully I am a morning person too.

Example One – A work day

Monday Schedule

5.00 – 6.00am	Wake and breakfast
6.00 – 7.15am	Get ready for School and work
	Clean up if time – put on washing and put in dryer
7.30	Leave for school and go to work
4.00pm	Return home from work
4.00 – 4.30pm	Get kid's dinner ready
4.30 – 5.15pm	Tidy up and do dishes, get kid's clothes ready for bed and dinner table ready to eat
5.15	Pick up kids from day care
6.00 – 6.15	Dinner
6.15 – 6.30	Clean up after dinner
6.30	Bath time – Steve (husband) baths the kids and Jackie to fold washing and put away

A Parent's Guide To Balance *And Getting More 'You' Time.*

7.00 – 7.30	Quiet time before bed with the kids
7.30	Kid's Bedtime
7.30 – 8.00	Do something from weekly cleaning list – sweep and mop floors
8.00 – 10.00	Writing time or Steve and me time

Example Two – Stay at home day

Wednesday Schedule

5.00 – 6.30am	Wake up and breakfast
6.30 – 7.30am	Breakfast clean up and get dressed for day, brush hair and teeth
	Put washing on for the day and hang out or put in dryer
7.30 – 8.30	TV off and Mummy playtime with kids
8.30 – 9.00	Morning tea
9.00 – 9.15	Clean up from morning tea
9.15 – 10.30	Kid's play alone time
	Jackie – Change bed sheets, vacuum floors, couches and under
10.30 – 11.00	Mummy playtime with kids
11.00 – 12.00	Get lunch ready and eat
12.00 – 12.30	Lunchtime and clean up

A Parent's Guide To Balance *And Getting More 'You' Time.*

12.30	Kids bedtime
12.30 – 2/2.30	Writing time or my time-out
2.30	Kid's awake and afternoon tea
3.00 – 4.00	Clean up afternoon tea then outside time
4.00 – 4.45	Prepare dinner
4.45 – 5.15	Group clean up with kids included. Folding washing and putting away
5.15 – 5.45	Dinner
5.45 – 6.15	Dinner clean up and get kid's clothes ready
6.15	Bath – (Steve to do)
6.45 – 7.30	Quiet time with kids
7.30	Kid's bedtime
7.30 – 10.00	Writing time or time with Steve

Example Three – A weekend day

Sunday Schedule

5.00 – 6.30	Wake up and breakfast
6.30 – 7.30	Breakfast clean up and get dressed for day, brush hair and clean teeth
	Put on washing and hang out, or put in dryer

A Parent's Guide To Balance *And Getting More 'You' Time.*

7.30 – 8.30	Do kid's day care lunches ready for Monday and Tuesday
8.30 – 9.00	Morning tea
9.00 – 9.15	Clean up morning tea
9.15 – 6.00	Flexi time – family outing, or no tasks assigned
6.00 – 6.30	Group clean up including folding and putting away washing and get kid's bed clothes ready
6.30	Bath
7.00 – 7.30	Quiet time with the kids before bed
7.30	Kid's bedtime
7.30 – 8.30	My TV Show – *Australian Idol*
8.30 – 10.30	Writing time or time with Steve

The examples above were created as a result of feeling unbalanced in the way I was running my life. Because I was inspired to grow my business I found I was spending a lot of time doing this and sacrificing quality time with my kids and my husband, which was not aligned with what I felt was important as the parent I wanted to be.

Then, if I was spending time with my kids or husband I felt I was sacrificing my business time and that was important to me too. I needed to create a plan where I felt balanced between my commitment to my family and my contribution to the successful flow of family life and my desire to pursue my personal goals.

I could've easily given up on what I wanted to do (my business) because I believed I 'should' be doing more housework or 'should' be giving more time to my family, but that wouldn't have made me feel fulfilled. I also could've decided to ignore what I "should" be doing and work on my business whenever I wanted to, ignoring the housework and the kids where possible. But that wouldn't have made me happy either. The consequences of that choice would've been living in a messy, cluttered house and living with unhappy children and an unsatisfied husband.

Neither of these two extremes aligned with what was important to me. Although my time to pursue my interests was important, so was my ability to raise happy, healthy children and maintain a loving successful marriage. In order to do both I had to arrange my time to be in balance with all of what was important to me.

Exercise Six – Create your own time schedule

Using your 'to do' lists and time allocations for each category (time out for me, quality time with the kids, quality time with your partner, household chores/errands,

work and miscellaneous (plus any additional categories you've had to add), formulate your own schedule that works for you for the next week.

You can even do this for the next month if you think things are not likely to change, however be flexible and don't be afraid to revisit it and move it around as life unfolds.

Remember, life doesn't always go to plan.

Summary to Part A – Managing your time

Part A of this book has been about learning strategies to manage your time effectively so you are living a balanced life that incorporates your needs, the needs of your family and the commitments you take on in your day to day life, whether that be work, housework, voluntary activities or personal pursuits.

The key points made through this section are as follows:

- Time management is not about time. It's about CHOICE and FOCUS. There is specific thinking underlying all stress and that thinking will always be in conflict with reality. You have beliefs about how life should be in order to feel valuable as a person and to enjoy life. This pursuit of pleasure and avoidance of pain is at the helm of all the decisions you make. By aligning your thinking with the reality based thinking model, you will alleviate stress and have the clarity to focus

A Parent's Guide To Balance *And Getting More 'You' Time.*

on the last three steps of the Mind TRACK to Happiness process.

- What is important to you? Effective time management will be obtained when you find balance between the day to day mandatory tasks you do and the things you consider are important. When you sacrifice what you consider is important you begin to feel stressed. What you consider important is often heavily attached to your beliefs about your worth. Although we know that you are always worthy you have a judging mind and your mind will judge with its habitual thinking lenses. To avoid stress, as well as reminding yourself of your true worth and the other reality based upgrades, it will also be helpful to align your priorities with what is fundamentally important to you.

- The brain always searches for evidence of what you give attention to. If you FOCUS on what you are missing out on you're not looking for solutions. You're only focussing on finding more evidence of what you are missing out on. When you FOCUS on your ideal life and how you want it to be, you start to find opportunities and pathways for getting it.

- Regularly create an updated schedule you can use as a guide to living a balanced lifestyle

A Parent's Guide To Balance *And Getting More 'You' Time.*

that incorporates all of your wants and needs. Regularly re-visit the schedule to make sure you are still on track to meeting your personal needs as well as the mandatory needs of everyone else.

In essence, time management is a plan that integrates all of the things you need to do with all of the things you would like to do. The key word here is 'plan'.

You cannot expect to achieve balance and adequate results with all of your parenting tasks and incorporate all of your personal wants and needs too without having a plan of how to do this.

However, the plan doesn't just happen. I hope by now you have seen there is a lot more involved in making decisions than just the conscious act of deciding.

This book has been an attempt to provoke you to think a little deeper about your life and how you CHOOSE to spend your time. Awareness is everything, so stay on top of consciously recognising your thinking and deliberately re-training your subconscious.

> "Definition of madness: keep on doing the same things again and again, expecting different results."
>
> Albert Einstein

A Parent's Guide To Balance *And Getting More 'You' Time.*

Part B – Time Out

A definition of time out according to the Free Online Dictionary is *'a pause from doing something (as work)'*.

We all need time out from anything we do in life. If we were to work full-time we would go home at night, put our feet up and idly watch TV, soothe our worries with a good book and a steamy hot bubble bath, or take a holiday somewhere fun or relaxing.

Regardless of how you would do this before becoming a parent, I suspect you probably took regular time out from your work.

Sometimes when we have been spent a lot of time around our partner, friends or family we also feel as if we need some space from them too – time out to step back from conflict or to just reconnect with your own thoughts. This used to be an easy thing to do before children – you simply walked away, or stop seeing them for a little while.

How often have you committed to a big project or have been in the middle of a difficult part of the project's process and said to yourself, *"I need to take a break and come back with a fresh mind."* And when you did that, how much better did you function after taking that break?

So why is it in every other aspect of your life it is okay for you to take a break, yet that's not allowed once you have

A Parent's Guide To Balance *And Getting More 'You' Time.*

children? If you do allow yourself time out why are you riddled with guilt?

Somewhere, somehow parents, and more commonly mothers, have become convinced our children must come first at all times and if we are to indulge in our own personal needs and desires we have become selfish and failing as a 'good parent'.

As we know, our beliefs were created as a result of our past experiences and influences, so I wonder what thinking is actually behind this 'rule' that time out is not allowed. Was it the indoctrinating comments people made during your first pregnancy that suggested, *"Your life is over now"* or *"You'll never get any time to yourself now you have children"* or *"You better save all of your money and have your fun now, because children will suck you dry"* or similar comments that you have taken on and accepted as truth?

Or perhaps it was the way you were raised. Perhaps your mother sacrificed everything, or so it seemed to you. Perhaps she did this because it made her life more fulfilling, or because it fulfilled the rules she was indoctrinated to believe. It just wasn't heard of that mums could do all the things that women do now.

I believe we are stuck in a generational gap. On one side we have been exposed to traditional gender roles, where the husband goes to work and the wife stays at home and plays mum. Her extra curricula activities centred round the home and domestic interests.

A Parent's Guide To Balance *And Getting More 'You' Time.*

On the other side of the spectrum we have the *'women can do it all'* message where we are taught we can and should have successful careers and do everything men do, although we've not quite let go of the domestic role and are getting very stressed trying to do both.

Men, on the other hand, haven't gotten off so lightly either. They too seem to be stuck in a generational gap of old ways versus new. Traditionally the bread winner and taking less of an active role in the raising of their children, dads are now under pressure to do more chores around the house, spend more time with the family and 'me' time seems to be slipping by the wayside for them also.

So it's not just women feeling the pressure.

What we *believe* earns us our 'good parent' badges is at the core of why we are not getting any time out. As we've established in the first part of this book, your time out actually doesn't have anything do with time.

Time is about priority beliefs attached to the agenda of pursuing pleasure and avoiding pain.

For example, if I feel like whenever I take time out from the family it impacts on my success as a parent, and that belief is stronger *in the moment* than the desire to take the time out, you will find yourself making choices to stay at home and sacrifice your time out.

However, parents who are able to pursue goals and interests outside of parenting, who aren't afraid to ask for help, have

A Parent's Guide To Balance *And Getting More 'You' Time.*

their children babysat and can figure out ways to get what they want, just believe their interests are valuable too.

As you've learnt with the first upgrade – life is a story of ups and downs, there is no right way for us to live our lives. Life is just a series of experiences, highs and lows, which lead to more highs and lows and none of these experiences are a reflection of your self-worth.

The parent who makes time for themselves versus the parent who doesn't is not a better or worse parent, they simply have different beliefs about time and self-worth. They are pursuing different pleasures and avoiding different experiences of pain due to these beliefs.

If your time for pursuing your interests is lacking it will be due to you making something else a priority. There will be something else you believe gives you more of a payoff – something that either makes you feel good, that you believe will define your character (self-worth) or give you something of value (rewards, accolades, a title or status of living up to an adopted label)

I know for some of you this can be a difficult concept to get your head around. Some of you reading this right now are resisting what I'm saying because your time out is due to seemingly unavoidable situations – for example, work combined with multiple children, combined with sports days, medical appointments, being a single parent and having no support. All of these are genuine issues that impact our time availability. I'm not disputing that.

A Parent's Guide To Balance *And Getting More 'You' Time.*

However, if you were to win yourself an all-expenses paid holiday to Hawaii, I bet you'd find the time to go.

If, in amongst all of your commitments, your best friend lost their partner or worse, their child, you would drop everything to go and support them and even go out of your way to make a few meals for the family or do whatever you could to help them out.

You make the time because you see it as a priority. You find a way to integrate this into your life amongst your usual rituals because it is a priority in the moment. It means something to you.

Is the reason you are not giving yourself time out because you just don't list it as a priority, or not priority enough in the moment for you to rearrange your schedule to fit it in?

The reality is you are getting a payoff for the activities you participate in that are overriding your availability for time out.

Readjusting your idea of time out

Often the reason we don't take a lot of time out is we have an old reference point of what time out is. Before becoming a parent time out meant holidays, a whole day to yourself, hours shopping or playing golf, or at the very least having an hour of uninterrupted time to read a book.

A Parent's Guide To Balance *And Getting More 'You' Time.*

It is not uncommon for parents I work with to get stuck in this old reference point and subscribe to the all or nothing mentality – if it can't be like it used to be then I can't have it at all.

We need to make a deliberate shift in how we think about taking time out because the reality is we don't live the same lives anymore. Our circumstances have changed and that means how we experience our time out has to change too.

A girlfriend once said to me, *"You figure out what you want to do and then you plot and scheme around the kids to do it."* This is what your new reality is now. You have to get rid of the old picture you have painted in your mind of how time out occurs in your life, and create a new picture that fits with present time reality.

When it comes to the time out you want to take nowadays, you may just need to do a little planning, or "scheming" as my friend suggests. Sometimes you need to steal your time out for a few minutes here or there or whenever possible.

The important thing is to embrace it when you have it.

Another friend of mine said to me once, *"But it just never seems to be enough"*. This is because you are looking through the missing out lens – the second lens on the stressful thinking model – focussing on what you're NOT getting or focussing on it not being enough.

You have to upgrade your thinking to be aligned with what you *are* getting and enjoy it in the present moment. You have to upgrade how you think about life when you aren't engaging in your personal pursuits and find the value in that.

What is your payoff for not taking time out?

You have the tools to be able to integrate time out now. Some of you may have even known these tools before you read this book, yet you still don't take the time out you need.

You know what you need to do. You may even know that it's good for you. Yet you still don't do it. Why?

Another good example of when we do this is smoking. We all know that smoking is bad for you, can make you sick and generally does nothing for good health whatsoever. Yet many people still smoke.

Why?

Logically they know they shouldn't smoke, however logic is not guiding this ship – the subconscious is. Logic lies in the conscious part of the brain. Habitual thinking lies in the subconscious.

Think of the conscious part of the brain where logic and conscious reasoning takes place as if it was the steering wheel of the car. The subconscious is the satellite navigation system.

You may logically know to take time out, or not to smoke, however it's the habitual thinking and all of those indoctrinated beliefs you have programmed in your satellite navigation system that are actually driving the car.

You may consciously steer your car to go north by telling yourself to head north (take time out), but when you lose awareness of your conscious thinking, the sat nav kicks in and steers you south (back to where habitual beliefs say you must do everything for your child, be the perfect role model, or whatever habitual belief is driving your priorities).

If you want to incorporate time out into your life and you feel like it's more than just a logistical case of planning, you have to take ownership. You do have a choice, it's just that the choice is coming from a sat nav that has attached your self-worth to something else.

In order to begin the process of change, we again need to follow the Mind TRACK to Happiness process.

Step One: Thoughts

This requires self-reflection. What is in it for you not to take time out? What other activities are you constantly making a priority and why? How have you attached your sense of worth to these other activities?

For example, in my earlier days of self-exploration after becoming a mum, I realised I would deliberately keep tabs on all of the things that had gone wrong during the day and

A Parent's Guide To Balance *And Getting More 'You' Time.*

work myself up over them so I could relay how terrible my day was to my husband when he walked through the door. Crazy, I know. Why would I do that?

Once I recognised there had to be a payoff somewhere for doing this, I realised the payoff was to get my husband to feel sorry for me and continue to help with the kids. I realised part of me (my subconscious) felt if I 'had it all together' this would give him a reason not to help.

I held onto the 'woe is me – I have it so hard' card in an attempt to control my husband's behaviour, unknowingly making myself miserable throughout the day. I needed evidence of my bad day so guess where my attention was? Looking for all of the bad things that were happening in the day. When you have your attention there you certainly aren't looking for the hidden good in the bad, or the value in your daily events.

Once I recognised this pattern of behaviour and its payoff, I was able to realise the craziness of it and put it to rest with the conscious mind. Whenever I became aware of myself doing it I would consciously steer my attention back to where I wanted it – looking for the hidden good.

My example just highlights how subliminal our habitual thinking can be and how easily it can send us south of the direction we consciously want to be heading in.

Here are some reasons why you may not be taking the time out you need and some of the habitual thinking behind it:

A Parent's Guide To Balance *And Getting More 'You' Time.*

- *If I don't take time out this will be evidence that I am a great parent. This means I will be a better parent than 'x' (friend, my parents, or my idea of the wrong parent) and people will think higher of me. The compliments and comments I get from others as a good parent make me feel good or will override the deep seated fear that I might actually be a bad parent* (the payoff – increased sense of self-worth: pursuit of pleasure).

  The trouble with this payoff is you don't end up looking like the good parent because you end up wearing yourself down, getting impatient and irritable and moving further away from your goal, winding up feeling even worse about yourself.

  Even if you do succeed to show this on the exterior, when you receive the compliments a part of you knows you are far from the ideal parent you would like to be. You still don't feel satisfied you have reached this goal, further increasing your stress and probably reinforcing that you need to spend more time in your parental role.

- *If I don't take time out I complain about it to my husband/friends/family and it makes*

A Parent's Guide To Balance *And Getting More 'You' Time.*

me feel special and important, because I have it harder than anyone else (the payoff – I get attention, feel loved and feel like I'm important when others sympathise with me – pursuit of pleasure through acceptance and acknowledgement).

This one is a common one, yet difficult to admit. We all like to feel special in some way and sometimes we've learnt to feel this way we have to get people to feel sorry for us. It can also be an unconscious ploy to get attention in order to feel loved, acknowledged or understood.

- *I cannot take time out because no one will do things the right way* (the payoff – I feel important because I'm the only one who can do these things properly or I have a belief that things have to be done a certain way in order to get my/my child's life right and stop me/them from missing out).

You can see here the pursuit of pleasure (feeling important) or the avoidance of pain (right life vs a wrong life) and all the things you or your child might miss out on if they have this wrong life. What do you believe it would say about you if they did miss out?

A Parent's Guide To Balance *And Getting More 'You' Time.*

Control issues are big contributors to stress about time. Sometimes a parent may become so attached to a certain way of doing things it becomes almost impossible to let go of the reins. The payoff comes directly from the right versus wrong lens, followed very closely by the missing out lens, all because of the belief the wrong way will mean a life of less value (the fourth lens).

Controlling life becomes the priority over taking time out, because time out might mean you lose control which would cause you pain (not physical pain, but discomfort) so you prefer to keep doing what you're doing.

Now it's your turn to reflect on some of your own circumstances. Why are you stopping yourself from taking time out for yourself? Consider what the payoff is for doing what you do and why it's a priority. How have you hinged your self-worth or pursuit of pleasure on these alternative activities? Or how are you avoiding pain from not taking time out (fears or failure or criticism?)

Remember, some of the answers to these questions won't be rational. Rational thinking is another function of the conscious. It's not rational to smoke cigarettes either. So be honest with yourself here.

A Parent's Guide To Balance *And Getting More 'You' Time.*

Allowing yourself to take time out

Once you become aware of the habitual pattern of thinking that stops you from taking your much needed time out, you can then move onto upgrading that thinking with Step Two of the Mind TRACK to Happiness process – Reality.

The reality is you aren't taking time out because you don't make it a priority or you have an incorrect perception of what time out should be based on old reference points.

If it is old reference points at fault you need to create a new picture of how time out occurs in conjunction with your present reality. If you have very young children the reality is life is fairly demanding for you right now and the amount of time out you have will be significantly different to what it used to be, or what it will be when they are older.

Using the four upgrades, there's a new story you need to tell yourself about time out in order to change your old reference points.

Life is a story of ups and downs

This is just a stage of my life. The reality is I will have fleeting moments where I will have some time to myself, for now. This is not a reflection of my whole life, it's just a part of it. Life is not better or worse right now, it's just a different set of experiences to what I'm used to. There are loads of good times in my life and there are some harder times in my life but they are all valuable to me. I will enjoy the moments of time out I get when they arise knowing they will come and go like *every* experience in my life's story.

Everything has value

I will look for the hidden good during the times when I'm not able to take time out. When I'm not having time out I'm still getting an experience of benefit to me. I have the experience of being a parent, bonding with my child, learning how to be more organised, learning about myself and how to handle difficult situations better, learning how to ask for help, or how to get better at something, and learning how to manage my time. I'm always learning something and having knowledge added to my life that serves me. I just need to deliberately look for it.

Priority Beliefs dictate behaviour (in any given moment)

There is no 'me' time. It's all my time and what I'm doing right now was chosen as a priority at some point because I believed in the moment of deciding it was important to me and gave me a payoff. The time spent in these activities is just as much a part of my life as the 'me' time I keep focussing on.

I may not always be doing what I want but I'm always doing what I believe to be in the best interests of myself. How I have rated my actions and choices is in direct alignment to what I believe it will mean about me to do each activity in my life.

A Parent's Guide To Balance *And Getting More 'You' Time.*

No matter what experiences I have, my life is always valuable

There is no experience that truly defines us or makes us more or less of a person. ALL of our experiences contribute to the knowledge we have, the lessons we learn and, consequently, how we contribute our unique selves to those around us.

You are always valuable whether you are taking time out or not. Your child's life always has value and the lessons they learn will inevitably contribute to others around them. Your child's life is not going to be less if you take some time for yourself. They are going to have experiences that shape their life with or without you.

Of course you want to be in their lives. That will always be a priority for you. But you don't have to be in every minute of their lives for their life to have value and vice versa.

A new way of thinking

Changing your thinking about time out and upgrading your habitual thinking is a process that will take time and conscious focus.

Using the analogy of your mind being like a car, you need to become aware of the habits of thinking programmed into your satellite navigation system (your subconscious) and consciously steer your attention towards the upgrades and a different way of perceiving life.

A Parent's Guide To Balance *And Getting More 'You' Time.*

When you continue to do that over and over again you begin to literally grow new neural connections in the brain and, as you repeat the new way of thinking, those neural pathways become stronger. The old thinking (and thus those neural pathways) become weaker and start to die off.

Essentially you will be consciously redirecting your attention towards the upgraded reality-based way of thinking. You will be physically reprogramming your satellite navigation system and soon enough you will find yourself habitually looking at life in this way.

The other really interesting thing about the brain and how it thinks is it is always looking for evidence – proof something is true.

Go back to the example of my ludicrous habit of finding all the bad in my day so I would get help from my husband. With my attention there, what did I find? Evidence of how bad my day was.

If you want to convince yourself it's okay to have time out you're going to need to find your proof. You need to give yourself evidence of the value that can come from time out – both for you and your family.

The more evidence you have that it's okay to take time out the more likely you are going to make it a priority.

So let's start to do that. Let's look at some reality based reasons why it's okay for you to take time out.

A Parent's Guide To Balance *And Getting More 'You' Time.*

Why you deserve time out

The obvious reason is because however chaotic it feels right now in whatever stage your children are at, you are still an individual with a thinking judging mind and you have preferences and biases.

From your experience to date you have things you enjoy doing more than others and it is our primal need to pursue pleasure, otherwise we feel like we are in pain and that brings a whole host of other unenjoyable experiences.

You didn't just lose that inherent need to want, desire and dream just because a little soul came along with big, and sometimes very loud and angry, demands.

If you have convinced yourself your wants and needs don't matter you are in conflict with reality. They do matter and if you try to neglect your joy, gradually you will find yourself feeling more unhappy and unfulfilled.

I think it's important to note here that in spiritual circles you are likely to be taught to be at peace in every moment regardless of what you are doing and this is a practice I am even teaching (and working on myself) in the *Parent's Guide to Mindfulness and Living in the Present Moment* ebook.

Mindfulness is an ongoing practice and because we aren't Buddhist monks that have been practicing the art of

A Parent's Guide To Balance *And Getting More 'You' Time.*

non-attachment for years, our present reality is that we have this judging mind that feels the need to seek joy in all activities.

You cannot neglect this present reality of your personal development or you will end up feeling more stressed and unhappy because you're not having any fun.

Neglecting your right to pursue activities outside of being a parent may eventually lead to anger, resentment, hatred and even depression.

It will lead to you spending more time rolling around in the stressful thinking lenses and finding it even harder to upgrade to our reality based thinking model.

Your brain will just keep finding further evidence that your life is wrong. That there is a right life and you're not living it. That you are missing out on a fun and enjoyable life. That you should be enjoying yourself and you should be able to think in a happy way. That you should be a better parent.

If you neglect yourself you may find yourself getting impatient or angry at the kids – not even close to the calm, composed image you have of this perfect parent. You resent the chores of being a parent and you generally make not just yourself, but everyone around you miserable and uncomfortable, all because you are trying to become a great parent who never neglects their child by giving herself time out.

A Parent's Guide To Balance *And Getting More 'You' Time.*

It's actually counterproductive not to take time out because it only produces the result of further stress, depression and anxiety.

The reason you deserve time out is not because you are letting yourself selfishly indulge in happiness, but because it is one of the key components to creating calmness, happiness and love, not just within you, but towards the family unit as a whole.

At least in the meantime while you are learning how to adopt that Buddhist Monk's ability for non-attachment.

The benefits of taking time out

So we've started to find some evidence of why it is valuable to take time out. I hope by now you are starting to form a good argument for taking that much needed space from your life as a parent.

Let me convince you even further as to why this is important to incorporate into your schedule.

Benefits for you:

> *Quality time out makes you feel like an individual.*
>
> It takes you away from 'just being a mum/dad' and helps you to realise you are a person. It helps you to maintain a deeper connection to

A Parent's Guide To Balance *And Getting More 'You' Time.*

the person you are. It helps you to see proof of your contribution to the world through interactions, friendships and being able to contribute your knowledge.

Although this is a missing out lens way of looking at things, it is often the case when we are with our children all the time, particularly when they are quite young, we don't get a lot of connection with others and that's what the habitual brain wants – to feel important, loved, acknowledged and a part of something.

Again, until you've attained that skill of being non-attached (which I don't believe anyone has every minute of their lives) this is an important understanding of the human mind.

Time out gives you other opportunities to learn and grow through experience.

By participating in activities outside of your parental duties you learn more about yourself and you learn more about experiencing life. When you experience life it builds character and adds meaning to your life. Again, you feel connected, loved and acknowledged. It's an innate need in our current development as human beings to feel like we are a part of the world in order to feel okay.

A Parent's Guide To Balance *And Getting More 'You' Time.*

Time out is great for your self-esteem.

Self-esteem is different from self-worth. Your self-worth is inherent. You are worthy because you exist regardless of your experiences. However, you have this judging mind that rates your self-worth. Self-esteem is your rating system – how you rate yourself in accordance with life's events. It comes from your learnt beliefs.

When you allow yourself time out you are often rating the experiences you are having highly and thus you feel good about what you are doing. You feel a sense of accomplishment and individuality – a step away from the robotic monotony of a life you have been rating as worth…less (which of course is not true based on upgrade 4 – your life is ALWAYS valuable).

Having quality time out generates a sense of peace and composure.

When you are rested, widened back, and personally fulfilled, you are naturally calmer, more tolerant and can maintain more perspective and patience. You don't tend to get so caught up in trivial events that would normally send you into a spin. When you are relaxed things like that don't seem to matter so much.

A Parent's Guide To Balance *And Getting More 'You' Time.*

Time out will help you to enjoy parenthood.

Often when you have spent some time away from your kids you realise how much you love them. This is important for them and for you. You appreciate seeing your little ones again and want to spend time with them after a break. If you don't have that break you forget how to appreciate them because they are always there.

Time out gives you head space!

It's a time to reflect, get some perspective, take time to upgrade your thinking and become more rational. A walk along the beach can often do this. If you are consumed and overwhelmed by life and are constantly being exposed to the things that cause you to feel consumed and overwhelmed, how is it possible for things to change? You need to have some space to look at the situation objectively from time to time, or just take a break from the situation altogether!

Benefits for your children, husband & you family:

When you are feeling more peaceful, refreshed, more rational and serene, you generate this energy to those around you.

When you take quality time out to connect with yourself and the things you like to do,

A Parent's Guide To Balance *And Getting More 'You' Time.*

your positivity and your renewed sense of self is reflected upon others naturally. It also allows you to be calmer, more patient and sincere with your children. This creates closer bonds, calmness and co-operation between all of your interactions.

When you take time-out and connect with yourself you are teaching your children how to respect themselves and their right pursue their interests.

I'm sure you want your children to grow up knowing that on top of the responsibilities they have in life, pursuing their personal goals is also important. You need to model this for them too. Often as parents we try to tell our children to do things we don't even do ourselves and then wonder why they grow up like us. They are watching your behaviour and learn off what you do as well as what you say.

When your children are not with you they are getting different experiences that help them to learn and grow.

Routine isn't always the best things for children at all times because it doesn't teach them resilience, flexibility and problem solving. If you had always experienced the same thing in the same way when you were growing up, would you have learnt the things you have? Haven't those times that were out of routine also taught you to do things you can now do?

You don't need to be in your child's life all the time for their life to have value. They will get other experiences from other people when you are not there, so time out will never make your child 'miss out' on their personal development. Sure they might miss out on an experience they wanted, but they never miss out on having an experience that helps them to learn and grow.

Have I given you enough evidence yet? Are you convinced time out is essential for you and your family's life to be happier?

Now we have looked at the reality of time out, we need to move onto the third step of the Mind TRACK to Happiness process: Aim – what do I want?

The different types of time out

Because life has changed since you became a parent, so too has what you want. Your goals are no longer what they used to be, or if they are the same the way you go about getting them will definitely have changed.

A Parent's Guide To Balance *And Getting More 'You' Time.*

It's important to assess some different categories of time out so you are recreating a new reference point to take into the solution focussed stages of the Mind TRACK to Happiness process – Aim, Choices, Know your plan and action it.

When you were reading the benefits of taking time out, you may have been wondering why you don't always feel the different benefits when going, let's say, to get a cup of coffee. Perhaps you feel like you just return from the one hour break straight back into the chaos you left behind and it's like it never happened.

This is because you need to be aware of and appreciate the different types of time out that benefit you in different ways, as follows:

The quick fix time out

This type of time out is designed to give you a quick break from being a parent. Think of it like a morning tea break from being a mother, or a lunch break from your job. Quick Fix Time Out includes:

- Doing housework when your partner or someone else has taken the kids away so you can do it uninterrupted. This type of time out allows you to think about things you want to while mechanically completing your chores. You don't have to participate in breaking up fights, getting three different sets of snacks and

A Parent's Guide To Balance *And Getting More 'You' Time.*

dealing with tantrums. It's not really time out in a traditional sense, but it can offer you some time to sort through your thoughts and gain some perspective on a situation. Plus you feel a sense of accomplishment at the end of it (before they all come back to make a mess again).

- Running down to the shop to get some groceries without the kids. Again this is not traditionally time out, as it is still a chore, but it can give you some time to think and calm down if necessary.

- Sitting down to a cup of coffee or your favourite TV show while the kids are asleep, even if it's just for 20 minutes. You get a few minutes to relax and unwind before the next shift begins.

Quick Fix Time Out is a very fleeting time out and not enough to generate the deep sense of peace and re-composure we have been talking about, but has its place in your life when things are really crazy and you are looking for a spontaneous and quick fix to avoid feeling consumed.

It's important to see the value in these times and to consciously acknowledge you are getting them so you can stop the 'whole world is bad' mentality from kicking in. Ups and downs, remember? Appreciating these little moments can help you remember the bigger picture.

A Parent's Guide To Balance *And Getting More 'You' Time.*

Refreshing Time Out

Refreshing time out is about rejuvenating your physical self which will make you feel better physically and keep you healthy, which in turn benefits you mentally and emotionally. These are:

- Catching up on sleep. This makes you feel physically better equipped to handle the world and your commitments. If you are lacking in sleep, this kind of time out is a necessity for being able to cope with raising your children calmly and in alignment with your goals as a parent. When we are tired it affects us physically, mentally and emotionally. Taking this kind of time out is imperative if you have a baby or an unwell, unsleeping child. The world is a different place to a well-rested parent.

- Get a massage, facial, manicure etc. This kind of time out is very relaxing and just what you need to soothe away your troubles momentarily. You awaken from these kinds of self-indulgences a new person physically, which has positive effects on you mentally and emotionally.

- Read a book or watching a movie. Sitting around idly and immersing yourself in a story is very relaxing and quite enjoyable. For moments in time you are miles away from your own life and relaxing into the realms of somewhere else.

- Have a long, hot bubble bath. This kind of time out is caring for the body. It relaxes you and can give you a renewed sense of peace and readiness to get back into your day to day life.

- Exercise. You just can't go past the feeling you get from a good workout. You feel so alive, focussed and energised, even when you've worked yourself hard. The feeling you get from regular exercise can go a long way towards how your respond to the various challenges of parenthood.

This type of time out is quite enriching on a surface level, and also has its place in creating a peaceful and balanced life for yourself.

Time out that recognises individuality

This type of time out is starting to move towards the core of who you are outside of being a parent. Time out like this allows you to take a break from your roles as a parent and reminds you there are other parts of you going on too. It's a time to recognise you are an individual with wants, needs and goals. Time out of this nature helps you identify your connection to life outside of the home and allows you to see you are not 'just a mum or dad'. You also have other

A Parent's Guide To Balance *And Getting More 'You' Time.*

interests outside of that role that make up who you are. Time out of this type is things like:

- Taking time out with your partner. Reconnecting as a couple is a really important time out activity. You are not just parents, but two individual people united as a team. Taking time out exclusively with your partner allows you to identify yourself as a loving couple and enjoy the relationship you have exclusive of the one you have together as parents.

- Coffee or lunch with friends. This kind of activity reminds you that you are a social being. Taking the kids with you for play with other friends' kids doesn't count in this category. This is exclusively uninterrupted conversation that is purely about you and the people you are socialising with.
When you do this you are remembering what it is like to connect to people other than littlies and enjoy their company in its purity. You also remember what it's like to eat an entire meal uninterrupted. Being with friends helps us feel accepted in the community and not isolated, which can sometimes be the feeling for a stay at home parent or a parent with a lot of demands.

- Attending social events, alone. Having fun is an essential part of time out. Doing something that makes you laugh, or smile or promotes real enjoyment of the activity cleanses your soul and your mind and helps to remind you of the individual you are. Being social helps you to be the person you are when you aren't thinking about your children's safety, toilet needs and meal times.

Time out recognising your individuality is starting to get closer to the core of how to feel more peaceful because it is about re-connecting with yourself and doing things that help you experience the bigger picture of your life. Parenthood is not the only experience happening on your life's journey.

Time Out for the Soul

Time Out for the Soul, in my opinion, is the most imperative form of time out you can give yourself. This time out will give you the core peace and calmness you desire. When you participate in time out for the soul, you will begin to find the time to take all of the other types of time out for yourself too.

When you experience time out for the soul your whole world feels more in balance. You feel like you have some perspective about life and the ups and downs you experience.

The kind of time out I am referring to in this area, is **Self-exploration** and **Meditation**.

A Parent's Guide To Balance *And Getting More 'You' Time.*

I highlight these two points here because I cannot express to you enough the absolute importance of adding these two things into your life.

Although I have been really interested in personal development since the age of 15 and have read many, many books on self-improvement, it was through an experiential personal development course called Avatar© that I experienced self-exploration for the first time.

Over a period of about two years I participated in experiential learning about myself and the patterns of my mind. I learnt a lot about the attachments I had to things and how those attachments made me feel. I have learnt about some of the unproductive dynamics and psychological games I have played with the relationships in my life. But most of all, I have experientially learnt to be completely, 100 percent accountable and responsible for the peacefulness in my life.

The most profound knowing I have achieved from continually practicing self-exploration is that **I** create all of the happiness and unhappiness in myself, regardless of whatever situation I come across because of the beliefs I have subscribed to.

On a surface level, this may seem to be a pretty obvious observation. It's pretty common knowledge these days that your thoughts create how you feel. However, knowledge is information and the application of this information is wisdom. When you understand the benefits of self-exploration and ridding yourself of those incorrect

A Parent's Guide To Balance *And Getting More 'You' Time.*

indoctrinated beliefs on an experiential level, rather than an intellectual level, that's when you REALLY become accountable for your life.

Self-exploration and the search for understanding why you are the way you are changes who you are from the depths of your being. When you truly know yourself – and I'm not just talking about knowing your strengths and weakness or your likes and dislikes, I'm talking about the core of who you are and why you do the things that you do – and you learn to accept the reality that you are a learning, growing human being who is never going to be perfect, you become at peace with yourself.

When you begin to explore the depths of your mind, you start to strip away the surface and superficial layers of your being (the ego – your incorrect beliefs about self) and you find a quieter, calmer and more compassionate person that has laid dormant in you all along, that you never even knew existed.

I learnt all of this before I had children, but still allowed myself to get sucked into blame, resentment and anger, and allowed myself to be consumed by all of those incorrect indoctrinations of how to be the perfect mum.

My habitual thinking about what I was missing out on as a mum consumed me and I was constantly feeling like I was giving up 'my life' and waiting for my children and my husband to behave in a certain way before I could achieve happiness.

A Parent's Guide To Balance *And Getting More 'You' Time.*

I had not thought about applying all the knowledge I had gained about myself previously to the area of being parent until I had my wake-up call – my angry outrage described in my book *The Happy Mum Handbook*.

After that time, when I was at the lowest and most depressed point of my life, I woke up and reconnected with the part of me that was conscious of how much my old programming (my satellite navigation system) was steering my life and I began to rebuild my contentment from the inside out by being deliberate about what I thought.

What I did in essence, from the depths of despair, is made a decision to find myself again, to rediscover that quiet, calm person I'd met a few times in my earlier experiences before becoming a mum.

Self-exploration is so important that you simply must make it a priority to do it. If there is a part of you reading this right now that is stirred up by what I'm saying to you, perhaps it's time to get started.

So many of the world's gurus, sages, saints and holy people of history have all said that same thing: *'Know thyself'*.

Self-exploration and an understanding of yourself is the key to freedom, peace and compassion for everyone, but you have to make it a priority to do so.

A Parent's Guide To Balance *And Getting More 'You' Time.*

Do it deliberately, experience the benefits of feeling happier, freer and living with more joy and you will give yourself enough evidence to want to make it a priority.

I believe it is even more important for parents in particular to embark on this journey of self-exploration, because here in lies the skills to teaching your own children how to live peaceful and happy lives.

Isn't that what everyone really wants for their kids – peace and happiness? Isn't that what *you* are ultimately looking for in your life?

Self-exploration is the key. Know yourself and you will experience peace.

Self-exploration is an on-going process. You begin somewhere, anywhere, perhaps this book is your starting point. Perhaps it's any of our products that continue to teach you how to understand yourself as a parent.

Begin to learn how to start peeling the layers off your ego – your indoctrinated beliefs about yourself – until you start to feel more connected to a deeper version of you.

This is not religious. It's not esoteric or a law of attraction type concept. It's just a feeling that begins to emerge when you realise just how much your thinking is in conflict with reality and when you align with your true self-worth. When you learn how to reprogram that satellite navigation system, you begin to FEEL differently about your life. You begin to feel more at peace.

A Parent's Guide To Balance *And Getting More 'You' Time.*

This can take some time, but the more you continue the easier your life becomes.

Time out for the soul is about giving yourself time to discover the new you.

Parenthood changes you physically, mentally, spiritually, morally, emotionally, and ethically. It effects every part of your being. Now is the best time to start handling all of these emotions of anxiety, depression and general unhappiness that sometimes come up when we have children.

All of those 'should've/could've' statements, the self-criticisms, the anger, the conflicts, the hurt, the judgments that are consuming your inner peace can be stripped away when you allow yourself Time Out for the Soul through self-exploration.

How do you begin to do this? You already have. If you are reading this far you have already begun walking your path towards inner peace.

You just need to start looking, 'choosing' to focus on finding the information to teach you how and do it.

At the Parental Stress Centre, this is what we focus on – teaching parents how to mentally and emotionally learn and grow and discover a personal peace that they can pass onto their children.

A Parent's Guide To Balance *And Getting More 'You' Time.*

Choices and Know your Plan and Action it – The two final steps on The Mind TRACK to Happiness Process

Our beliefs on how to be a good parent often outweigh the desire to indulge in personal pursuits. It becomes a priority to do everything for our kids and nothing for ourselves, but often as we have discussed, it takes us further from our goal.

By now you it is my hope that you can see the reason you haven't been taking time out for yourself has little to do with time and more to do with your beliefs about what your other activities mean about you and your life.

I'm hoping by this stage you also realise you can 'have your cake and eat it too'. There can be balance between time out and being a supportive, great role model for your children. It's just a matter of planning and action.

That is what the final two steps are about.

If you haven't done so already, go back to Part A of this book and do the exercises on time management. Create a schedule that incorporates all of your commitments, while factoring in some time for yourself as well.

This may mean you need to push some other things to the backburner, but now you are aware that time management is about priorities you can consciously ask yourself what your payoff is for making one thing a priority over another and whether that reasoning is in alignment with the reality based thinking lenses (the upgrades).

Sort out what you want, in terms of time out that addresses each of the time out areas. Find ways to incorporate Quick Fixes every day. Try to incorporate refreshing time out activities several times a week. Make time out for your individuality a weekly or bi-weekly thing and take time out for your soul as often as you can – daily, hourly, by the minute. This ongoing deliberate effort will result in changes to your life you never thought possible.

Conclusion

One of the most important missions for a parent is learning how to juggle everything – the kids, work, family commitments, social activities, and pursuing your own personal interests.

This book has only just touched on some of the fundamentals of being able to feel like you are meeting all of these demands in a way that aligns with your integrity and desires.

This is an ongoing battle for many of us, which is why self-exploration is the key to unlocking happiness and personal peace.

The reality is the world is getting busier. We do more, want more and take more on and as a result we seem to have less time.

A Parent's Guide To Balance *And Getting More 'You' Time.*

Understanding that priority beliefs govern behaviour you can now take a step back and assess what's really important to you.

If one particular activity is stopping you from experiencing more of what you hold important to you, it's because you've made it a priority to do that activity.

For example if your working life is overtaking the time you'd like to spend with your children, then work has been made the priority over your children. This may be a reality of right now, but it doesn't have to be a reality of your future with research, planning and action.

Don't allow yourself to subscribe to thinking change could never happen to you. Of course it can. You just may not have the knowledge right now to do it.

Follow the Mind TRACK to Happiness process for anything you desire in life. If time out or anything to do with time management is struggling to meet your ideal, rather than sticking your head in the sand and wishing it wasn't so, or rolling around in the stressful thinking lenses and feeling bad about it, start recognising the thinking that has put you there in the first place.

Begin today by acknowledging the payoffs, the indoctrinated beliefs, the incorrect attachments of your self-worth to your achievements that have brought you to your current situation and start aligning your thinking with the reality of life (the upgrades).

A Parent's Guide To Balance *And Getting More 'You' Time.*

Start thinking about what you want and stop focussing on what you're not getting. Learn about what your choices, options and solutions are for creating what you want and start working on your plan today.

Life is about Choice and Focus, but not in its traditional context.

Focus comes from priority beliefs. Whatever you put your attention on is what your mind will find evidence of.

Keep rolling around in how little time you have to pursue what you want and you'll keep finding evidence that you don't have time to pursue what you want. You simply don't have the attention left to focus on getting what you want when you are looking through this lens.

Keep changing your habits consciously to make new decisions, arming yourself with the right information that reinforces your new direction and take action.

These are the steps that will not only see you managing your life more efficiently, but will also help you to feel more at peace in the process.

All life's experiences are valuable and there is no one way to get life right. Your worth on this planet is intrinsic and there is nothing you have to be, do or have to make you more valuable than you already are. Your worth is un-compromise-able.

A Parent's Guide To Balance *And Getting More 'You' Time.*

So with this in mind, life now becomes about what you want to experience, not what you have to in order to be deemed important to the world.

So what do you want? What experiences would you like to have, as an individual, as a couple and as a parent?

Decide what you want to experience in this lifetime and then find the evidence and information that will help you to achieve it.

Prioritise your life in accordance with what is important to you and be conscious of when you are getting consumed with the idea of life needing to go in a perceived 'right' direction.

Keep programming that satellite navigation system to pay attention to what you want and how to get it and soon enough you will find you think this way by habit.

Time management is not about managing your time, it's about being conscious of your priorities governed by your beliefs. Manage them to be in alignment with reality and how you want your life to look and you'll create for yourself a whole different experience of how to live.

PARENTAL STRESS CENTRE

www.parentalstress.com.au

The home of

- Sign up for our monthly newsletter
- Read our blogs
- Find many more helpful products
- Find out about Author -Jackie Hall's public speaking appearances, book signings, seminars and workshops

For daily tips and inspirational quotes

www.facebook.com/pages/parentalstresscentre

www.ingramcontent.com/pod-product-compliance
Lightning Source LLC
Chambersburg PA
CBHW071455160426
43195CB00013B/2121